CHILDREN'S MINISTRY
IN THE WAY OF

DAVID M. CSINOS AND
IVY BECKWITH

FOREWORD BY **JOHN H. WESTERHOFF III**

IVP Books

An imprint of InterVarsity Press
Downers Grove, Illinois

InterVarsity Press
P.O. Box 1400, Downers Grove, IL 60515-1426
World Wide Web: www.ivpress.com
E-mail: email@ivpress.com

InterVarsity Press® is the book-publishing division of InterVarsity Christian Fellowship/USA®, a movement of students and faculty active on campus at hundreds of universities, colleges and schools of nursing in the United States of America, and a member movement of the International Fellowship of Evangelical Students. For information about local and regional activities, write Public Relations Dept., InterVarsity Christian Fellowship/ USA, 6400 Schroeder Rd., P.O. Box 7895, Madison, WI 53707-7895, or visit the IVCF website at <www .intervarsity.org>.

All Scripture quotations, unless otherwise indicated, are taken from the Common English Bible. *Copyright ©2011 by Christian Resources Development Corporation. Used by permission. All rights reserved worldwide.*

Unless otherwise indicated, the stories in this book are true. Some names and identifying information in this book have been changed to protect the privacy of the individuals involved.

"Disciples-in-Training" words and music by Bryan Moyer Suderman. ©2002, 2011 SmallTall Music (www .smalltallmusic.com). Reprinted by permission.

Cover design: David Fassett
Interior design: Beth Hagenberg
Images: circle of life: © Patricia Marroquin/iStockphoto
  alphabet and numbers: © Heike Kampe/iStockphoto
  red texture: © gary milner/iStockphoto

ISBN 978-0-8308-4108-0 (print)
ISBN 978-0-8308-6468-3 (digital)

Printed in the United States of America ∞

Library of Congress Cataloging-in-Publication Data

A catalog record for this book is available from the Library of Congress.

P	19	18	17	16	15	14	13	12	11	10	9	8	7	6	5	4	3	2	1
Y	29	28	27	26	25	24	23	22	21	20	19	18	17	16	15	14	13

For Jenny,

my copilgrim in the adventure of life.

D.M.C.

To all the children who

have populated all my churches:

thank you for teaching me,

inspiring me and giving me hope.

I.B.

Contents

Foreword

❑ ❑ ❑

CHILDREN'S MINISTRY IN THE WAY OF JESUS is a significant, fresh and engaging resource for all those who are concerned about children and the church's learning and teaching ministry. I therefore was delighted and honored to be invited to write its foreword. Aware that we live in a transition era in Christianity's history in the West and that the theological and educational foundations of learning and teaching need to radically change in order to address these new times, this book explores and recommends relevant and imaginative means for the church to fulfill faithfully its educational ministry in a new day.

As a theologian of educational theory, I have for more than fifty years been engaged in an attempt to understand the Christian faith and life, contemporary educational theories, and the historical, social and cultural context in which we live as believers in Jesus Christ and members of his church. I therefore will begin this foreword with a few words about my understanding of our contemporary context.

The history of the Western church can be divided into a number of eras and transitional centuries. For example, we can speak of the apostolic age (the first four centuries), Christendom (which lasted from the fourth to the tenth/eleventh centuries), the Middle Ages and, beginning in the seventeenth century, what has been known as modernity.

Between each of these historical eras there were transitional periods, each of which had distinguishable characteristics that influenced and were influenced by theology and educational praxis. The

Middle Ages, or the age of faith was followed by a period of transition known as the Protestant Reformation and the Catholic Counter-Reformation which, in the seventeenth century, became modernity, or the age of reason. This is the era we know best, and while each era has value, each has limits as well. Beginning in the twentieth century, a transition to something new has begun to emerge. It is referred to as postmodernity, which is a time of radical change in every aspect of our lives. Some find this transitional time exciting, and others long to return to more stable times.

Transition times are difficult to live in. Old, familiar understandings and ways of doing things are dying, and new understandings and ways have yet to be born. It is for some a pregnant time of hope and opportunity. New understandings and possibilities are waiting to emerge. It is experienced as a time to explore new theologies and new educational theories and practice. For others it is experienced as a time of dislocation and loss. Some desire to return to a past that never was, are critical of all attempts at change and refuse to even consider theological alternatives, a new Christianity for a new day.

Much of our theology and practice in Christian education has either been dominated by the acceptance or rejection of modernity. Liberal Christians have accepted uncritically the characteristics of modernity, while conservatives have tended to simply reject modernity without providing any real alternatives. Because of modernity's emphasis on reason and biblical historical-critical method, conservative fundamentalists have argued for anti-intellectual biblical literalism. From my perspective modernity and its assumption that it is a witness to human enlightenment has reached its moral limits, and fundamentalism could not and cannot provide any insights for the future.

Many of us who are Christian educators have concluded that we have reached the limits of modernity's values and need to develop and experiment with alternative understandings and strategies. Which I hope explains my enthusiasm for this book.

Consider how mainstream Christian educators have tended to place an emphasis on reason and the intellectual way of thinking and knowing while neglecting revelation, the imagination and the intuitive way of thinking and knowing. We have neglected the centrality of the arts (dance, drama, poetry, music and the visual arts) and replaced it with the science of technology.

During modernity we have increasingly turned the world and everything in it into an object for our investigation and manipulation. The social sciences tend to turn people into objects to study and shape. Similarly, we have turned the Bible into an object for study rather than a subject that addresses us. Increasingly we have understood human beings as autonomous individuals who through analytical reason and disinterested judgment can make rational decisions. We have so emphasized the freedom of the will that we have neglected the influences (not determinants) of heredity and environment, and the spiritual influences of good and evil. Further we have forgotten that we by nature can do nothing without God's help, and that God has chosen to do nothing without our help. We are dependent beings who only can abide in the difference God has made and is making.

We also face tremendous changes in the social and cultural contexts in which we live and work. For example, the family and the roles of men and women are radically changing. Our society and our schools are becoming increasingly secularized and polarized. Multiculturalism, religious pluralism and globalization are influencing all our social institutions. Daily we are confronted by new social, moral and spiritual challenges. Theological systems and liturgical expressions are in search of new, more relevant manifestations. And Christian education as we have known it is no longer viable. Dave and Ivy are aware of these challenges and have in this book begun to address them.

It is, however, important to remember that what may appear as new has historical precedent. Christian educators in the 1900s began to work on the problems that now face us. The theologians I studied with in the 1950s provided a foundation for my work on Christian nurture, which appeared in my first book, *Values for Tomorrow's Children* (1970), to be followed by my major work *Will Our Children Have Faith?* (1976), now in its third revised and expanded edition including a new memoir. In those works I contended that the schooling (context)-instructional (process) paradigm that dominated modernity was no longer useful. I advocated a community of faith-nurturing (socialization) paradigm to replace it. It is this paradigm that undergirds and informs *Children's Ministry in the Way of Jesus*.

Believing that in postmodernity children are being ignored by a new important emphasis on adults, Dave and Ivy have focused on the church's ministry with children, especially in this time of transition, change and challenges facing the church and the world. They have achieved their goal to collect and share ideas and practices for children's ministry in families, congregations and communities that are committed to the discovery of more relevant and contemporary expressions of Christian faith and life.

In order to provide a theoretical foundation for their emphasis on children in the church I turn to my book *Bringing Up Children in the Christian Faith* (1980). In 1900 Ellen Key proclaimed the twentieth century to be the century of the child. For hundreds of years childhood was unrecognized and children were simply little adults. During modernity, the Enlightenment era, childhood was discovered. It was a mixed blessing, for now they were seen as mere children and not complete human beings.

Typically, we explain that children do not know enough and cannot think well enough, feel deeply enough or act maturely enough to be treated equally with adults. Moreover, children are considered well-adjusted if they are malleable to the adult will and maladjusted if they resist it. The majority of studies of children fit into the category of "problems" and deal with how we should do this or that to children or for children.

The discovery of childhood often implied that children are not valued for what they are, but only for what they can become. There was a tendency to describe children as dependent, nonrational and nonproductive (they play). Adults, on the other hand, are independent, rational and productive. Children were seen as having no value in themselves; rather they needed to be made into adults.

Metaphorically, children were either like valuable pieces of raw material that need to be shaped or formed by adults into their predetermined design (we are to do things *to* children), or like seeds that need to be cared for by adults until they become full grown (we are to do things *for* children). A better metaphor is that children are like pilgrims, copilgrims with adults in a shared journey over time (we are to do things *with* children). As St. Paul suggests, on this journey children will need to give up their childishness. But, as Jesus suggests, adults need to become childlike.

Dave and Ivy, aware that the Christian Scriptures, like the Christian tradition generally and even much of contemporary culture, express a deep ambivalence about children, offer a fresh biblical and theological approach to bringing up children in the Christian life of faith. Their well-written and expansive work provides evidence that our communities of faith have much to learn from children's experiences of God and views of the world, especially through nature, the arts and ritual. By valuing the perspectives of children, they address quite different questions from those that have typically dominated much of Christian education, especially among some conservative evangelicals.

Dave and Ivy bring a theologically sound, broad perspective to the church's ministry with children by placing an emphasis on faith, character and consciousness. Faith, for example, they understand to be perception or how we view life and our lives rather than a rational acceptance of propositional truths or doctrines. Further, they acknowledge that the opposite of faith is not doubt but certainty.

Similarly, character is a concern for the habits of our hearts or behavioral disposition that undergird our moral decision making, rather than a blind acceptance of particular teachings about right and wrong.

And consciousness is that mental state that makes possible particular experiences such as the presence and action of God in our lives rather than a demand for some particular pious conversion experience. Consciousness involves reflecting on experiences that focus on our spiritual lives of growing in an ever-deepening and loving relationship with God that manifests itself as the moral life of discerning and doing the will of God.

Dave and Ivy are aware that catechesis, the making of Christlike persons and communities, is comprised of three, lifelong, interdependent, intentional nurturing processes: formation (the participation in and practice of the Christian life of faith), education (critical reflection on all of life and our lives in the light of the gospel), and instruction/training (the acquisition of knowledge and skills foundational to the Christian life of faith); formation being a dominant concern for ministry with children and instruction/training and education being dominant with adults.

Acknowledging the centrality of baptism and the lifelong process of living into the reality of our baptism, they have helped us to understand that baptism tells us the truth about ourselves as children of God and brothers and sisters to each other. By baptism, we become *a Christian* (noun) and then we spend the rest of our lives becoming *Christian* (adjective). Regretfully, because of inadequate Christian learning and teaching, many persons who are by their baptism a Christian never become Christian in mature ways.

Now if any of these personal insights of mine, insights I found imaginatively addressed in this book, entice you to reflect on your understanding and practice of Christian education and formation in a new day, read on. You will not be disappointed. Indeed, you will be enthusiastically pleased. I was!

John H. Westerhoff III
Episcopal priest, author, lecturer, resident theologian at
St. Anne's Episcopal Church in Atlanta, and professor of theology
and Christian nurture (retired) at Duke University.

Acknowledgments

◻ ◻ ◻

WHEN WE FIRST DECIDED TO VENTURE into these waters and write this book, we wanted to make sure that it found the right home. We are so pleased that InterVarsity Press opened their doors to us when all we had was an idea and some handwritten notes resembling an early table of contents. Thanks especially to our editor, Dave Zimmerman, for his dedication to the project and for providing feedback to improve it along the way.

Writing this book has been a labor of love, and in the process we have welcomed friends to join us by reading early drafts and making helpful suggestions. Amy Dolan, Brian McLaren and Jenny Csinos took the time to thoroughly read the manuscript, affirm its importance and recommend how to make the book better.

The words within these pages come from experiences we have had in many different churches, conferences and conversations. From the children in our ministries over the years to the friends in the field, thank you for allowing us to walk with you in the way of Jesus.

Neither of us had coauthored a book, and we walked through the door of joint authorship with excitement, anticipation and some trepidation. But we have been overjoyed at the opportunity to collaborate on this project, and it has been an honor for us to bounce ideas off one another, revise and rewrite together, and create something we are both incredibly proud of. So we thank each other for the courage and risk it took to work with one another, to pour our hearts and minds out to the other and trust that our ideas will be held up by each other as sacred trusts.

Introduction

Doing Children's Ministry Differently

Look! I'm making all things new.

REVELATION 21:5

◻ ◻ ◻

L AKESIDE **COMMUNITY CHURCH IS CHANGING.** When it began over twenty-five years ago, the five families that embarked on this church plant met in a local community center in the suburbs of a mid-sized city in North America. Their goal was to "bring God's message of salvation" to their city, often through community outreach programs. Over the years the church grew and grew, and blueprints were drawn up for a large auditorium and a gymnasium to replace the original sanctuary, which would become the children's and youth ministry wing.

A few years ago one of the members of Lakeside's pastoral team became interested in conversations surrounding how to reimagine and expand common understandings of what it means to be authentic followers of Jesus in the twenty-first century. He shared a few books and blogs with his senior pastor, who thought that the authors had some good points. The senior pastor wondered if Lakeside had been losing touch with the culture of its city, even though it had always sought to be "relevant." Armed with a book budget, he searched through the virtual shelves of online booksellers for more resources about how to engage contemporary culture while remaining faithful to a commitment to follow Jesus.

And these two pastors weren't the only ones starting to see things differently. As they were becoming energized by their searches for new ways of being the church and following Jesus, so were others in the congregation. Eventually, after careful consideration and countless board meetings, Lakeside Church decided that the time was right for beginning a missional offshoot in the downtown core of their city. The new group, iChurch, aimed at making a larger impact in the city and connecting with a new demographic of potential members.

Led by a seminary-trained, hip-hop-loving pastor in his mid-thirties, iChurch attracted a number of young couples, many of whom had children. The fact that the community met in a coffee shop meant that people who had been disenfranchised or skeptical of more mainstream churches could find a place where they were more comfortable.

For the most part this new missional gathering focused its energy into reaching twenty- and thirty-somethings in their city's gentrifying downtown core. Anticipating that some of these young people would bring along their children, they hired Marvin to be iChurch's part-time children's director and began renting a room for children's ministry in an art gallery across the street from the coffeehouse.

The young children's director was commissioned with running a program that would reflect the missional, forward-thinking vision of iChurch while teaching children what it means to be authentic followers of Jesus in today's world. Marvin searched high and low for a curriculum based on the sort of values that iChurch embraced, but came up dry. Without the time and budget to develop his own curriculum, he began looking for books and online resources about children's spiritual formation with new forms of Christianity so that he could adapt a more conventional yet readily available off-the-shelf program to suit his community's particular context and needs.

Marvin uncovered a few blog posts and read some recent books about ministry with children, but he was still overwhelmed with the daunting task of developing a program that nurtured children in this new faith community. Where was he to turn for ideas and support? Many of the children's ministry resources that he'd been encouraged to use by the leaders of iChurch and other children's ministers actually reinforced theology and practices that the leaders and members of this new faith community were questioning and moving beyond. It seemed like literature about new ways of being disciples and resources for children's ministry were worlds apart. Marvin began to wonder if children even have a place within the burgeoning conversation about how to be disciples in the world today.

Across the pond Sheila was also beginning to raise important questions about children's ministry. As the director of children's formation for a diocese of the Church of England, she was responsible for overseeing children's ministry throughout the region. She was known to pass along a magazine article or recommend a podcast to children's ministers and leaders, and she was always on the prowl for innovative ways to nurture children's spiritual lives.

One unusually warm spring day a few years ago, she made her way to a large urban church to attend a lecture by a North American pastor who had been experimenting with expanding understandings of and practices for following Jesus, and had written a few books on the subject. She found herself wanting to stand up and shout "Amen!" or "That's right!" as the speaker talked about how the church needs to make the shift from modern to postmodern ways of being disciples of Jesus. "After all," he said, "as much as some people decry the word *postmodern*, we live in a postmodern world. We need postmodern churches and postmodern faith."

At the end of the lecture Sheila rushed to the microphone that was eagerly waiting to take questions from members of the audience. When it was her turn to speak, she introduced herself as the director of children's formation for the diocese and asked her question: "How do the sorts of shifts in culture and church that you spoke about affect how we do ministry with children here in the UK as well as in other parts of the world?"

The speaker paused for a moment, seemingly caught off guard by Sheila's poignant question. "That's such a great question," he replied.

"And it's one that I've thought about many times. Unfortunately, I don't have an answer. And I don't really know if I'm the right person to offer an informed response to your question. I do think that children are important members of the church—this is something that I've come to believe more and more since becoming a parent a number of years ago. But I think that people like you—innovative leaders who are committed to kids and who are knowledgeable in areas such as formation, education and theology—you're the ones who can lead us in a revolution in children's ministry, a revolution that helps us better form children into disciples of Jesus. So, please, search for a response to your question. And when you find one, let me know what it is, because the future of children's ministry—and the future of the church—depends on it."

Sheila went back to her seat filled with energy and passion to explore ministry with children in this time of transition, change and challenge in the church and the world. She went home and immediately began ordering books that the speaker had mentioned in his presentation so that she could understand these new forms of church that are sprouting and growing around the world. She knew that a number of people in her diocese had started a "pub theology" group that was geared at discussing Christianity amid current cultural shifts like postmodernism, postcolonialism and globalization. She began attending their gatherings and visiting churches that were exploring innovative and fresh ways of doing and being church.

Over the next several months Sheila wrote articles for Anglican magazines. She began a blog about new kinds of children's ministry, and compiled a short bibliography of resources about children's ministry and contemporary forms of church. And all the while she reflected on and experimented with how to do children's spiritual formation in ways that reflected the expanding theology, practices and values that she was coming to develop. She approached the diocese for funding to develop a curriculum for children's education that was appropriate for churches and other ministry leaders who were making similar shifts in their views and practices of Christian faith, yet remained faithful to her Anglican tradition. With each step on this journey Sheila was reinvigorated with an energy that was contagious to the children's ministers in her diocese. Within a few years she had changed the face of children's ministry in the Church of England through infectious spirit and her curriculum, "Come to Me."

CHILDREN'S MINISTRY IN THE WAY

These two fictional scenarios mirror situations we've encountered and stories we've heard from folks in many parts of the world. And to a degree we see ourselves in Marvin and Sheila. Change is happening in the church as clergy and laypeople ask important questions about the shape of theology, ministry and the Christian faith in contexts characterized by profound cultural shifts. Resources abound that describe and prescribe these movements to reexamine and rediscover faithful Christianity in many corners of today's world.

In the past number of years we have been involved in churches and broader conversations that are intentionally seeking to explore new ways of following Jesus and helping others do so in our present age. Through our involvement in these churches and through talking with many others who are on similar journeys, we have discovered that current models of children's ministry don't always fit in these forward-looking faith communities—there's a disconnect between what adults are learning and doing and what children are learning and doing in the very same congregations.[1] And this worried us. In the words of Melvin Bray, "I don't know that we can have a new kind of Christianity if it's just for adults and [if] we don't find a way to pass our faith and our faith traditions, these new faith traditions and rituals that we're creating, along to our young people. It'll die on the vine."[2]

This made us think about what children's ministry in the "way of Jesus" (children's ministry that is faithful to the teachings and life of Jesus) might look like in churches and in other ministry contexts that join us in our frustration over this disconnect. What would this type of children's ministry value? How would this sort of children's ministry view children and their places within the church? How would this kind of children's ministry teach the Bible, deal with children's questions and nurture relationships? This book is the outgrowth of these questions and the experiences and discussions that they sparked.

But as we envisioned children's ministry in the way of Jesus, we also realized that it had implications for all kinds of churches and contexts. As we shared ideas in this book in conversations with colleagues and in presentations at conferences, we were overwhelmed to learn that children's ministers, Sunday school teachers, camp leaders and parents in all sorts of churches and from all over the world are wrestling with the same questions we wrestled with on our journey to write this book. We realized that the concepts, ideas and practices we share in these pages have implications for anyone who is truly interested in the helping children love God and live in the way of Jesus.

We see this book as a collection of ideas and practices for children's ministry in communities, congregations and families that want to help children grow as disciples of Jesus. It's sort of a guidebook for children's spiritual formation within churches and communities who are expanding their understandings of what it means to follow in the way of Jesus. As we seek to remain true to the conversations and ideas surrounding faith and ministry in our contemporary world, we realize that what matters most is faithfulness to Jesus and the way of faith and life that he shared through his words and actions. An exciting and innovative approach to ministry is worthless if it diverges from the peace, love, wholeness and restoration inherent in the gospel, and if it does not educate and encourage children to become authentic and faithful disciples of Jesus.

This book is not a systematic, comprehensive, universal handbook for a particular new kind of children's ministry. We don't want to imperialistically impose our way of doing ministry with children in every church. This book is a collection of practices, approaches and ideas that are contextually situated and limited by our experiences and perspectives. Our hope is that they can be lifted by readers and adapted to all sorts of contexts and circumstances in ways that are appropriate to the particularities and nuances of readers' initiatives in children's spiritual formation. Some people may find some of our ideas helpful in their ministry as pastors, parents, teachers or lay leaders. Others might find that some ideas may not seem like a good fit for their contexts.

Some chapters may inspire you to begin experimenting with new ways of doing children's ministry. Other chapters might make you want to throw the book across the room. Either way, we invite you into a conversation about forming authentic young disciples of Jesus.

GUIDING ASSUMPTIONS

Before we jump into chapter one, we want to share a few assumptions and beliefs that have been front of mind as we've written this book.

Many paths on a common quest. There's been a surge in the past decade or two of folks who are trying to move the church forward, folks who are writing, ministering and speaking about how to be Christian in the world we find ourselves in. As it has always been throughout the history of Christianity, people in all sorts of denominations and contexts are expanding their views and practices surrounding what it means to follow Jesus in our world here and now.

Our experiences have taught us that while many of these people are on a similar quest, there are different roots that are being planted and different branches that are sprouting. As followers of Jesus have set out on journeys to reimagine church and faith, they've taken all sorts of new paths. Some leave well-worn trails and bushwhack, breaking with old traditions and forging new ones in the process. Others trace their steps backward and reflect on where they have come from and how to reinvigorate their church, denomination and faith tradition. Others still courageously venture out on paths that may be new for them, but are really trails older than the hills through which they wind.

As we've written this book, we haven't had one particular path in mind. Instead, we've tried to remain true to the broader quest shared among all these pilgrims. We find pockets of vitality in all sorts of places, from churches breaking new ground on their journeys to live in the way of Jesus to age-old denominations that may seem to grow dim as they struggle to retain members, but are really waiting for a phoenix to rise from the ashes of former flames. So whether an Anglican diocese like Sheila's is seeking fresh ideas for doing church, a group of folks who aren't part of established churches are gathering at a local pub for sessions of "theology on tap," or a band of renegade Catholics or Baptists—or, better yet, Catholics *and* Baptists together—are meeting together to explore how to live as authentic Christ followers in today's world, children's ministry in the way of Jesus matters.

Gathered and scattered. What is church? Ask ten people and you might get a dozen answers. For some, church is where people attend worship services. For others it's a community that gets together to encourage and support one another on their faith journeys. For others still church is an organized religious denomination, like the Presbyterian Church or the Ukrainian Orthodox Church.

We believe that the church is all of these things and more. We have a very broad view of church, one that makes room for all sorts of ways that Christ followers gather and scatter in the world. So when we speak of the church, we aren't just referring to Roper Street United Church and to the official practices and activities that occur there. We're referring to all the ways that we as followers of Jesus are the church, as individuals, families, NGOs, community organizations, denominations and, yes, even local churches.

Sometimes people assume that we speak and write primarily for our fellow pastors and leaders in the frontlines of congregational ministry, those who teach Sunday school, mentor children and adolescents, develop programs for children's spiritual formation, and who never miss a children's pastors' conference.

And while we certainly have those involved in congregational ministry with children in mind, our imagined audience is much broader. After all, we have a broad view of church, and as you'll see in chapter one, we have a broad view of ministry with children. At times throughout the writing of this book, we've pictured senior pastors and youth ministers flipping through pages for insight into children's spiritual formation; parents who want to help their kids grow into authentic, thoughtful disciples of Jesus; schoolteachers looking for ideas for enhancing spiritual education, religious education, character education or citizenship education with children; and grandparents, aunts, uncles and godparents hoping to help young family members grow into responsible Christ-followers who love God and their neighbors.

With this broad intended audience we've tried to write in ways that connect with all sorts of people who are interested in children's spiritual formation. We've tried to cast our nets wide as we share ideas that we hope can be translated into many contexts as all sorts of people seek to form young people into authentic disciples. But we do so out of our experiences in children's spiritual formation, which have usually taken place in the context of faith communities.

Sporadic involvement. The days of children and families coming to church on a regular basis are over. We can't assume that children are going to show up every week, that their parents are going to bring them to every (or even most) church activity. In a presentation a few years ago, sociologist of religion Reginald Bibby asked a large group of ministers to raise their hands if they considered two Sundays a month to be a good turnout for even the most committed families in their congregations. There weren't too many hands that weren't in the air.

With this in mind, we believe children's ministry needs to become more than just Sunday school, church services and midweek programs. While we value these traditional forms of ecclesial life and, as you'll see, we believe that children need to be part of them, children's spiritual formation can't rely on Sunday mornings to form authentic disciples of Jesus. After all, church is more than Sunday services!

Pastors, parents and teachers need to become more creative and innovative in their approaches to forming children, looking at how to make a significant impact in the lives of children who have won perfect attendance pins and those that are only nominally involved in local parishes. We hope that what we offer in this book will spark ideas for how you can nurture the spiritual lives of children in whatever context you minister—in families, local churches, camps, schools, community centers and all other places where children's spiritual lives are nourished.

A *starting point.* Finally, it's been our assumption all along that this book is not the final word on children's spiritual formation in the way of Jesus. We're simply responding to a need that we've observed for some time, a need for better approaches to nurturing children's spiritual formation within families and faith communities seeking to follow

Jesus in today's world—and thoughtful resources that can help people on this journey.

This book is a starting point—a springboard for bouncing ideas off one another. There is always more to say. There are always better ideas, better concepts, better practices that ought to be shared. It is our hope that this book will generate new ideas for new generations of Christ-followers—that it will spark fresh approaches for forming young disciples.

For Better Formation, Let's Do Children's Ministry Differently

In a 2012 article Donald Stuss lamented the disconnection between medical research and treatment. It takes much too long for research in the medical field to evolve into outcomes for patients.[3] The solution, in his view, is to do science differently.

How do we do science differently? Stuss shares four elements of emerging approaches to medical research. First, patients need to have meaningful roles in how their treatments are developed. Second, scientists need to see all research as part of a continuum or web, with the more basic aspects affecting those that are more complex. Third, researchers need to become interdisciplinary, and researchers in different fields, institutions and specialties ought to work together. Finally, scientists and those in industry need to collaborate early in the research process.

This short article highlights how valuable it is to think creatively, to try new approaches and test out new ideas. And the four ideas Stuss offers can be adapted for improving Christian formation. We continue to hear so many people involved in ministry with children and youth (and adults) lament about how difficult it is to get children interested, to keep youth involved in church and to connect Christ with the rest of their lives. And almost everyone seems to have their own opinions about the person, attitude or model that's to blame for these problems.

But maybe medical researchers aren't the only ones who need to do things differently. Maybe to do better spiritual formation, to form better disciples of Jesus, we need to do children's ministry differently.

1

The Task of Children's Ministry

I fell quickly for the man with the lamb—dreamy Jesus.
You know the one, with the long locks and the deep blue eyes. . . .
But he was not a three-dimensional character in my life.
He lived in a picture on my wall.

JANELL ANEMA,
"Confessions of a Sunday School Superstar"

▣ ▣ ▣

IVY WAS LEANING ON THE COUNTER in the work room of the Midwestern church where she was the children's pastor, reading a flier from a large Southern California megachurch advertising a conference it was holding on church growth. A seminar on children's ministry caught her eye, so she continued to read the description of that seminar, expecting it to be about training volunteers or how to have a nursery that young parents would drool over. Instead, this seminar was about how to make sure your children's ministry programs were attractive to outsiders so these programs could be a way to market your church to the community. This was, in the mid 1990s, the first time she'd come across this idea of turning children's ministry into a tool for marketing a church rather than a means to the spiritual nurture and formation of children.

This idea of using children's ministry to market churches doesn't sit well with us. We've seen similar scenarios played out time and again in church marketing materials and in conversations with children's pastors. Children's ministry is often seen first and foremost by senior pastors, executive pastors and church leaders as programs that will attract more people into their churches—not as places that play a role in helping children learn to love God and live in the way of Jesus. If the programs are top-notch and kids find them fun, parents will return to this church because they won't have to fight with their youngsters to go to church every Sunday morning—so the gist of this thinking goes.

Ivy couldn't escape this thinking, even then, at her well-run and thoughtful church. She had to run her respective programs, even if she did not have the volunteers to staff them.

For example, the summer before Ivy resigned from this church, she was having a difficult time staffing her mid-week programs. Several long-term volunteers had stepped down that past spring, and while their resignations had not been totally unexpected, these people were difficult acts to follow—and everyone that Ivy asked to step in knew this. As August came, she had several age-level programs without leaders and the looming deadline of the Wednesday after Labor Day when, come proverbial hell or high water, every program had to begin. Otherwise where would the people who came to prayer meetings, divorce recovery, choir rehearsal or Bible classes put their children? Ivy really didn't know what she was going to do. She was a pretty good children's pastor, but she couldn't manufacture competent adult leaders out of thin air. Even if she could have found subs, the quality of the programs would have suffered.

Ivy was again confronted with this attitude when she began a ministry position at a fairly large mainline church. While trying to provide an environment and experiences conducive to the spiritual formation of children, the senior minister really only wanted her to be providing experiences that were so much fun for kids their parents would forgo their weekends at their ski houses in lieu of church school. Part of the problem was that the church had the money to have a bouncy house and pony rides every Sunday, if so desired. Ivy chose not to spend the money that way, but was under constant pressure to do so.

Our point in telling these stories is to show that some churches become intent on creating programs for children in order to provide undergirding for other church ministries and become more attractive to children and parents than the church down the street. When this happens, churches lose what it means to truly be involved in ministry with children. The idea of the "killer" program becomes more important for church leadership than what actually happens in the program. Guided by assumptions in our consumer culture, the primary question becomes not, Are the children growing spiritually? or, Are kids becoming better disciples of Jesus? but, Do the kids and the parents like it enough to come back? Now, we believe that church programs for children can be fun, attractive and spiritually nurturing. We don't believe these things are mutually exclusive. However, the idea of attractiveness seems to take a back seat to how we think about ministry to children and how spiritual formation happens for children in the community of faith.

A (Brief) Recent History of Children's Ministry

How did this happen? Why can it seem like more churches want to meet the consumerist needs of children and parents so that they don't have to pull out their hair to get their children in the minivan and through the doors of the church than meet the spiritual and relational needs of young people as they help them to be formed in faith?

Perhaps the modern era has provided breeding ground for an attitude in some churches and adults that children's programs exist to serve the needs of the adults in the congregation and make the church attractive to families in the neighboring community. Parents and pastors alike may love the church nursery and preschool programs because they eliminate noisy young children from worship services and provide a respite from the constant care that infants and toddlers require. Adults are more apt to attend midweek or Saturday programs if they have some place to drop off their children for free. More and more families let their children choose a new church based on their experiences in children's ministry.

But throughout most of the history of the church it has not always been this way. Puritans and their children sat through worship services of three hours or more each Sunday, and John Wesley decried the advent of church programs for children, saying that these programs were usurping the parental responsibility to spiritually nurture one's own children. Midweek church programs for children are relatively new phenomena that took shape in the 1950s primarily as outreach programs to unchurched or underprivileged children. But sometime in the late twentieth century the importance of church growth was touted by ministry leaders and speakers, and children's programs became vehicles for church growth and keeping children and adults separate—not for being environments for providing experiences of spiritual formation and nurture.

But these aren't the only reasons why so many churches have bought into a program-based children's ministry rather than a spiritual-formation-based children's ministry.

Early in the twentieth century churches became enamored of changes that were happening in the world of secular education. Christian educators began to think about ways these new ideas about school could be translated into congregational religious education. If these new methods could teach math and history better, why couldn't they also do a better job of teaching children to be Christians? Church school curricula were revamped and countless faith communities began to hire (mostly) men with seminary training in religious education to be ministers of education and administrators of these church schools. This formal schooling-instructional model of children's religious education worked for churches for a while because volunteer teachers were often willing to teach every Sunday and attend training meetings. Churches were committed to providing good schools for their children.

As the twentieth century progressed into the 1940s, some churches became disenchanted with the official church school curriculum provided by their denominations. Teachers began complaining that it was boring for the children and often difficult to teach.

Henrietta Mears, the minister of education at Hollywood Presbyterian Church in Southern California, took these complaints seriously. She began to write her own curriculum for her congregation, usually rising early each morning to write lessons before she went to work. Other churches began to hear about the success she was experiencing with this curriculum and wanted to use it too. Luckily for her and those who wanted to get their hands on the fruits of her labors, she had family members in the printing business. They began to print and sell this new curriculum, and Gospel Light Publications was born.

Other independent curriculum publishing companies born during that era have similar stories. Curriculum changed, and churches and their educational staff members continued to work to provide better congregational school programs for their children. And it worked. But again, teachers were often highly committed to these programs, teaching every week and being willing to go for training. A great example of this is Gospel Light's International Center for Learning, which had its heyday in the 1970s. These teacher-training conferences began on Thursday nights and ended on Saturdays. Volunteer teachers attended the conference in its entirety.

Another example of this is the Sunday School Convention movement. From the 1940s through the 1980s, many major cities in the United States hosted large yearly convocations of volunteer Sunday school teachers. These well-attended gatherings were held at large conference centers all over the country. Some of these training events still exist today, but through the 1990s and into the twenty-first century their popularity and attendance diminished.

But through the late 1970s and 1980s the baby boomers were coming of age and having children of their own—and they had different ideas about what church involvement meant. They weren't as willing to commit to teaching every Sunday and didn't always see the point in vigorous teacher training. There was also a growing willingness to pay for things to be done for them and for their children. If they could fork over money for people to teach their kids ballet, why couldn't they do the same for folks to teach their children to be Christians? The church staff position of children's pastor took off, and ministry with children became professionalized.

Churches were still attempting to do good schooling with a revolving staff of volunteer teachers who were too often minimally trained in how to teach children and work with the assigned curriculum. This was a recipe for school done poorly—and this is often what happened. But we're sure many readers can attest firsthand that bad school (unprepared teachers, teachers with little relationship with their students, teachers with no knowledge of classroom management, teachers who aren't really committed to good teaching) is a recipe for bored children and for a Sunday school where little learning—let alone spiritual formation—takes place.

While this was happening in local churches, two things were occurring in the wider church which would turn into tsunamis of change for the world of Sunday school and children's ministry. In 1974 Thom Schultz produced the first issue of *Group* magazine in his garage. And in 1975 Willow Creek Community Church held its first official service in a movie theater in Palatine, Illinois. That first issue of *Group* magazine would eventually become Group Publishing, and Willow Creek Community Church would spawn a wide-reaching children's ministry model called Promiseland. Both developments would significantly change the face of church-based children's programming.

When Group moved into developing children's ministry curricula and resources, they did their homework and discovered that a lot of churches were, indeed, operating out of a schooling-instruction model—and not doing it very well. They identified the problem as one of methodology. What child after sitting in school all week wanted to come to church and do the same thing, only this time with Jesus-themed worksheets and rote learning about the Bible? Group proposed instead an experiential education model in their Hands-On Bible Curriculum. The curriculum had children playing games, it included a box of toys called "gizmos," and it promoted a theory of "active learning."

Willow Creek determined that in order to be seeker-friendly, they needed children's programs that matched what they were doing in their worship services. They wanted their weekend children's ministry to be "the best day of the child's week." So they created children's programs that eschewed the traditional one teacher-one class schooling-instructional model in favor of a large group-small group model with volunteers as small group leaders and large group leaders pulling the church's small group model into the children's ministry. They also incorporated nonbiblical presession activities and a band to provide lively music into their learning environments.

And churches were watching. Many of them were frustrated with their current models of children's programming and saw what Group and Willow Creek were doing as both something that could be successful for them and as breaths of fresh air. Children's ministry leaders flocked to Promiseland conferences held at Willow Creek in order to learn the secrets of their success. Group saw huge interest in their new books and curriculum products.

But implementation of these new ideas wasn't as successful as some hoped it would be. For example, much of the success of Promiseland was in the fact that volunteers in each age group became a tight, bonded small group who met weekly, not just for planning but for building relationships and community with each other. The children's ministry leaders at Willow Creek were able to pull this off, at least partly, because the church had an overall ethos of small groups. Everyone in the congregation was encouraged to be part of a small group and this was hammered home each week in the worship and teaching services. So someone taking this important component of Promiseland success back to a church without this communal ethos of the importance of small groups might have had a difficult time conveying the importance of this weekly commitment to the volunteers in his or her church. And one reason why Promiseland had success was because all of the components (small groups of volunteers, music, skits, etc.) were designed to work together and grew out of the greater ethos of Willow Creek Community Church. It was difficult to replicate the success they had without all of the parts working, without all the gears turning together to drive the ministry machine. It was, after all, designed specifically for Willow Creek.

Early adapters of Group's Hands-On Bible curriculum had great success with it. Children seemed to love the "gizmos" and the games. And it appeared easier to use than more traditional curricula. However, what ended up happening was that, like any other curriculum, the lessons required teachers to do a degree of preparation, and a basic understanding of experiential education was needed to lead the lessons effectively. This in turn required volunteer teachers to attend training sessions. As more churches started to use this curriculum, training seemed to happen less and less. Once again, churches were holding poor versions of school—only this time it was more visible because badly done experiential education can quickly become chaotic.

Whether churches are practicing experiential education, using small group-large group models, or ministering in traditional teacher-centered classrooms, most programs still attempt to engage in spiritual formation and nurture of children through schooling methodology. Churches still rely on programmatic understandings of children's ministry. One can jazz it up with gizmos, games, movies, music and any manner of child-friendly chaos, but in the end it still ends up being school. It still ends up being just another program for children. If a church is really interested in authentic spiritual formation with children, it will do well to look past the newest program on the shelves and past thinking about spiritual formation in terms of schooling-instructional models.

A WIDE VIEW OF CHILDREN'S MINISTRY

In the end, ministry isn't really about school (even church school). And it's not really about midweek clubs, Bible quizzing championships, vacation Bible school, children's church, the latest curricula and church-based day camps. While these and other programs can easily define children's ministry in the eyes of some, children's ministry at its best isn't really about programs.

It's about ministry.

But what exactly is ministry? This word is frequently used in congregations, theological books and pretty much any other place where Christians are found. *Ministry* is used so often and to speak of so many sorts of things that it can quickly lose its meaning. But what do we mean when we use this term? What *is* ministry?

A quick search in an online dictionary reveals a variety of meanings associated with this word. It can refer to clergy, that is, "a body or class of ministers of religion." It can also refer to the functions performed by clergy. But these definitions don't seem to be appropriate for many churches we've known, particularly those that uphold relational ecclesiologies (church formed by relationships and community rather than organization and structure). So using *ministry* to denote the functions of a "professional" class of ordained clergy seems to miss the mark.

So we ask again: What is ministry? To move toward a sufficient answer, we turn to a small theological dictionary titled *Crazy Talk* that proves that theological education and formation can indeed be fun.

> Ministry \MIN-nih-stree\ n.
>
> An office instituted by God for work in God's world, the holders of which often spend too much time in their offices.
>
> With an unfortunate assonance with *misery*, the office of *ministry* was instituted by God for the alleviation of misery but, unfortunately, sometimes causes it. The purpose of the office is to minister to the needs of others, to love, save, and bless the world. Sadly, the temptation is for holders of the office to see first to the needs of the office. But here is the incredibly good news—God has chosen to use sinners in order to love, save, and bless the world. Which means we are all qualified for ministry.[1]

Other understandings of *ministry* are also helpful in nailing down what we mean when we advocate for children's ministry. In some definitions the word *service* is often associated with ministry. Ministry can mean service that people perform for the betterment of others. The Greek word *diakonia* is the predecessor of our modern English word *ministry*. In its original Greek, *diakonia* means service and caring for one another. So we see once again that ministry refers to service for the betterment of other people. Ministry exists to help people form, develop and live healthy, flourishing lives. So although theological dictionaries may see ministry as a noun, it's also a verb. Ministry is about ministering. It's about action for the betterment of others.

Children's ministry, then, isn't really about building fun and entertaining programs for children so parents will be able to attend church without being interrupted. It's not about adding names to rosters of Sunday school classes, day camps and midweek programs. It's about serving children, caring for them and forming them into people who serve one another and the world in the way of Jesus. This, after all, was what Jesus' ministry was all about!

There is certainly room in this understanding of children's ministry for programs. But we run into problems when programs define ministry, when the flourishing of programs comes to trump the flourishing of children. Programs can certainly be part of serving, of forming holistic, flourishing, healthy lives. But they shouldn't dominate what it means to do children's ministry. Our retrospective look at children's ministry over the past number of decades shows that ministry can easily be seen as synonymous with programming, with school-like models for offering children a fun place to be taught and offering parents a respite from the stresses of raising a family.

Children's ministry is about service—not programming. But even this simple notion can become problematic. In our contemporary consumer/capitalist society, children can easily be seen as consumers of ministry, those who are on the receiving end of ministry. Notions of ministry *to* or *for* children can denote this view of children's ministry, one of adults actively ministering and children passively consuming ministry. It's reminiscent of Brazilian educator Paulo Freire's naming of "banking education," a model that sees students as passive receptacles that teachers fill with information of their choosing.[2]

But churches can join others who are moving toward ministry *with* children, ministry that involves serving children, being served by children and serving the world with children. Faith communities that hold fast to relational, nonhierarchical and equalizing ideals are poised to raise the banner for ministry *with* children. The adult serves, the child serves and children's ministry happens when young and old serve and receive the service of others.

This is the task of children's ministry.

Our discussion of how school-like models and programs to children can usurp the true meaning of ministry—serving and being served by young people in the Christian faith—isn't unique to us. In the 1970s renowned theologian John Westerhoff made a similar observation about the bankruptcy of what he referred to as a "schooling-instructional paradigm" for religious education.[3] He argued for the enculturation of children into the community of faith, for walking with children on the spiritual journey and for understanding being Christian as "being open to learn from another person (even a child) as well as to share one's understandings and ways."[4] This is ministry with children in the finest sense of the term.

Westerhoff believes that questioning a programmatic, schooling-instructional approach to children's religious education offers great opportunities to rethink what it means to educate children, to form children into young disciples and to allow our journey of discipleship to be formed by children.[5] Children's ministry can endeavor to create a formational environment for children, not a school-like, programmatic environment. It can move away from being about providing child care support for adult programs or about attracting more people into the church. Children's ministry can become *ministry with children*, ministry that provides experiences within the faith community that lead them to a greater love of God and to practice living in the way of Jesus.

Clearly, we have a wide view of what children's ministry is. We see children's ministry as more than just midweek programs or Sunday school classes in church basements. We see children's ministry as more than teaching children about God, the Bible, church and Christian living.

For us, children's ministry is anything and everything we do to serve children as they walk on the spiritual journey. Children's ministry is all that we do to care for the whole of children's lives—mind, body and soul. Children's ministry is all of our efforts to nurture the spiritual formation of children, to help them live in the way of Jesus, to support them on the journey of being disciples of Christ.

So when we use the term *children's ministry* (or *ministry with children*), we refer to all those ministerial practices and activities that are done with children. As you'll discover in the pages to come, ministry with children happens when adults of all ages form friendships with young people, when we work to ensure that all children—regardless of age, ability, culture, race, gender, class and family life—receive radical hospitality, when we worship as a congregation with young people as active and meaningful participants, when we engage in theological (and even nontheological) conversations with children, when we take their questions seriously, and when we link arms with young disciples to work for justice and care in the world.

Children's ministry isn't merely providing cognitive input about that one moral or theological point each story or lesson was meant to teach. It's not about helping children fall in love with the "dreamy Jesus" portrayed in their Sunday school workbooks. It's about helping them live as committed disciples of the radical way of life Jesus calls us to.

Children's ministry is less about providing children with absolute answers and more about helping them live faithfully with questions and doubts that arise on the journey of discipleship. It aims at nurturing the whole life of the child and not compartmentalizing the child's "church life" from the rest of the child's life. It realizes that children feel God's love when they are surrounded by a close-knit faith community who loves them and sees them as valued participants. It realizes that children make the values of God's reign their own by seeing them lived out radically in their churches and homes—not simply by learning about them in a classroom or through a programmed activity. It understands that children are learners *and* teachers, and that they have as much to teach adults about life in God's kingdom as we adults have to teach them.

Jesus said one must become like a child to enter God's kingdom. We take these words seriously as we seek to minister with children.

2

Authentic Spirituality

Childhood is openness. Human childhood is infinite openness. The mature childhood of the adult is the attitude in which we bravely and trustfully maintain an infinite openness in all circumstances and despite the experiences of life which seem to invite us to close ourselves. Such openness, infinite and maintained in all circumstances, yet put into practice in the actual manner in which we live our lives, is the expression of man's religious existence.

KARL RAHNER, "Ideas for a Theology of Childhood"

WHEN DAVE FIRST SIGNED UP FOR FACEBOOK, he was fascinated by friends—both old and new—who described their religious beliefs as "spiritual, with no affiliation" or "more spiritual than religious."[1] And when he created a Facebook account a number of years ago, the "spiritual but not religious" phenomenon was just taking shape. Now it seems to be common nomenclature, one option among many for describing one's religious and spiritual life.

Respected researchers and writers like Robert Wuthnow, Christian Smith, Reginald Bibby and Diana Butler Bass have discovered that young people—whether or not they're part of an established religious tradition or community—are placing an emphasis on spirituality.[2] For a while we heard about clergy who fretted about their perception that young people are embracing spirituality while rejecting religion. But the truth is that in labeling themselves as "spiritual," younger generations aren't necessarily throwing out the proverbial baby with the bathwater. Many are opting for spirituality *and* religion.[3]

But regardless of whether younger generations describe themselves as religious, they tend to distinguish between spirituality and religion. While spirituality and religion were once synonymous in many contexts, young people are increasingly seeing them as separate (yet related) phenomena.[4]

Back to Facebook. It's been a number of years since Dave signed up for Facebook and discovered how many friends placed an importance on spirituality in their (religious or nonreligious) lives. Now he's learning about their growing families. Several of the people he's friended over the years have had children, have partnered with people who have children or have adopted children. He wonders how his friends will pass this emphasis on spirituality on to their children. For some this will mean embracing both religion and spirituality—they'll baptize or dedicate their children *and* encourage them to have personal spiritual experiences. For others spirituality may come to trump and overshadow involvement in religious traditions and communities. But whether their families bring them to religious services every week or once in a blue moon, this younger generation is being raised by a generation of parents that by and large distinguish religion and spirituality.

SPIRITUALITY AS WE UNDERSTAND IT

Over the last few decades there's been a surge of books, blogs and resources dedicated to the topic of human spirituality. Many groups and task forces have formed to specifically discuss issues involving the spiritual lives of children. But despite this wealth of information it's still difficult to find consensus about what exactly spirituality is and, more specifically, what someone means when they talk about children's spirituality. In fact, it seems like the more groups form, conferences develop and books are written about the topic, the more difficult it becomes to nail down a definition of children's spirituality. After all, how can anyone define something as abstract and intangible as the human spirit? But while it can't be pinned down for detailed observation, it's possible to sense what it means to be spiritual and what the spiritual life of children looks like.

Noted children's spirituality scholar Rebecca Nye says that spirituality is like the wind—"though it might be experienced, observed and described, it cannot be 'captured.'"[5] Jean Vanier, founder of L'Arche, made a similar observation: "we can hear the wind—maybe even feel it on our faces—but we don't know where it's coming from or where it's going. So it is with things of the Spirit. You don't quite know where you are coming from or where you are going."[6]

This uncertainty about the human spirit has led thinkers and researchers to study how spirituality is experienced in human beings. Many believe that spirituality is an inherent aspect of the human condition; they argue that all people are born with spiritual capacities. And this fundamental dimension of our lives can be seen more clearly in children, who enter the world—to use the words of Catholic theologian Karl Rahner—with an "infinite openness"[7] to the spiritual life.

Believing that spirituality is more easily perceived in the lives of young people, Rebecca Nye set out to study the spiritual lives of children in Britain. After meeting with children who were six and ten years old, and racking up over one thousand pages of interview transcripts, she felt that she could confidently describe children's spirituality as *relational consciousness*.

Basically, Nye's conversations with children from different religious backgrounds led her to see that they all possessed a certain spiritual quality of life, a consciousness or an awareness that went beyond simply being alert or attentive. To use the words of eighteenth-century theologian Jean-Pierre de Caussade, this consciousness is "the sacrament of the present moment."[8] It's a keen awareness of the presence of the transcendent. In Christian terms it's a full awareness of the presence of God—not just knowledge about God.

This is where the relational quality of relational consciousness comes in. The full awareness involved in spirituality is an immediate awareness of relationship—a "sense of felt connection" to one's self, other people, the material world and, ultimately, God.[9]

In *The Spirit of the Child*, Nye offers a few case studies of how relational consciousness was manifested in the young people who were part of her research. Six-year-old Ruth, for example, showed a profound relationship with nature, one that included "a strong feeling of connection to the natural world as something that was full of gifts for her and deserved her respect and love in return."[10] It was a reciprocal relationship of giving and taking, and taking and giving, with nature. And what is more, she had a profound sense or consciousness of this connection, and it infiltrated her religious imagination. In describing heaven she drew from her connection with nature, likening it to the sense/consciousness/awareness of a spring morning.[11] For Ruth nature is the divine locus of her spiritual life.

Like Nye's work, the research of Barbara Kimes Myers has had a significant impact on how to make sense of spirituality, especially in young people. She understands spirituality as the process of transcendence. From the Latin for "to climb over," *transcendence* refers to going beyond the limitations of our present, here-and-now realities.[12] Whether learning, praying or simply wondering about the mysteries of the world, children are capable of "climbing over" the horizons of their present knowledge, environment and reality. Transcendence isn't a one-time event. Although it can be manifested in conversion experiences and other particular spiritual incidents, it is an ongoing process that occurs throughout the lifespan.

Myers describes the transcendental nature of the human spirit through the example of Daniel, an eleventh-month-old child.[13] As he sits in his high chair with his lunch on the tray before him, Daniel reaches onto his plate and picks up his peas one by one. Grasping the tiny vegetable between his fingers, he leans his body forward and proceeds to drop it on the floor, carefully studying its descent to the ground. Then he reaches for another pea and continues this experimentation. For Daniel, studying how he can make his peas fall to the floor below him is a process of transcendence — it involves testing the limitations of his body and the world around him, and seeking to push beyond what he thought he once knew about his capabilities and the nature of the world in which he lives.

So while it's impossible to nail down a once-and-for-all definition of *spirituality*, we can get a sense of what spirituality is. Drawing from Nye's idea of spirituality as relational consciousness and Myers's view of transcendence, it's possible to describe this innate, biological aspect of the human condition as a relational connection to the living God that is beyond our understanding and reality. This transcendent God showers all people with grace by giving us the immeasurable gift of the capacity to know God, to sense the very presence of God and to enter into a real, life-forming relationship with God. Of course, this view has its limitations. But it helps us gain some conceptual clarity about an ineffable aspect of the human condition and allows us to move forward throughout this book from a common understanding of what it means to be spiritual.

WHAT'S RELIGION GOT TO DO WITH IT?

So if spirituality is an awareness of our relationship with God, what exactly is religion? In many cases, *religion* is broadly defined as an array of beliefs about the origins and nature of the universe, often involving rituals and devotional ceremonies, and including some sort of ethical code that governs human conduct. Other definitions might describe religion as the practice of a set of religious beliefs or a group that adheres to a specific set of beliefs and practices.

So religion has to do with the intentional and often structured ways that people express and live out their spirituality. It involves beliefs, practices and communities.

First, religion deals with how we understand our relationship with God. This is the realm of religious beliefs. As human beings attempt to make sense of God, the world and ourselves, we codify our understandings as more appropriate or accurate ways of comprehending God, one another and life in general. In the process, texts have been written and held up as authoritative or divinely inspired records of how humanity has encountered and interacted with God in various eras, cultures and contexts. Different religious groups have formed around agreed upon beliefs defining what they hold to be the best ways to explain their relationship with and sense the presence of God.

Second, religion involves what we do to feel God's presence in our lives. While we can certainly have divine encounters with God apart from religious traditions, a religious group forms a consensus about which practices its members will use in order to foster these encounters. Whether through musical worship, foot washing, Communion, abstaining from certain foods, wearing particular garments or engaging in certain forms of prayer, members of religious traditions use practices to foster their spiritual lives, that is, the awareness of their connection with God.

Finally, religion is about community. Religions are composed of groups of individuals who have agreed on specific ways of understanding God and connecting with God. There's no such thing as a religion of one. Beliefs and practices that are part of religious traditions are held by groups of individuals who agree that these beliefs and practices are the ways they can best make sense of and become aware of the transcendent in their lives. Religions are only religions when they involve multiple people who affirm ways of understanding and expressing their spiritual lives.

So while spirituality is the general term for our immediate awareness of God's presence, religion is an attempt to codify and generalize these personal experiences in order to understand them and to help people have these experiences. All human beings are born with a spiritual capacity, but not all people are religious. While we've heard some people denounce religion in favor of a "pure" and "personal" spirituality, being part of a religious group or tradition is a common way to express one's innate spirituality. Even though spirituality is important, religion matters too.

At the beginning of this chapter we mentioned folks who describe themselves as being "spiritual but not religious." Lately there has been discussion both in the Christian media and more secular outlets about these people who embrace spirituality while rejecting religious traditions and communities. While some researchers find that young people are choosing spirituality *and* religion, other descriptions of the millennial generation often refer to them as being spiritual but not too interested in organized religion. Recent research from both the Pew

Foundation and the Barna Group show that some teens and young adults can be critical of the institutional church—and of Christianity in general.[14] But if both spirituality and religion matter to spiritual formation, then those of us who minister with children need to pay special attention to encouraging children to embrace that innate interest in God and helping them see real connections between their spirituality and the rituals and relationships of a faith community/tradition.

NURTURING THE SPIRITUAL LIVES OF CHILDREN

We are born with a spiritual capacity. We all come into the world with an ability to connect and relate to ourselves, one another, the world around us and the very God who created us.

Over time, however, as children learn how the world works and about the reality of life around them, young spiritual pilgrims might begin to close themselves off to sensing God's presence. The gift of spirituality that is so vital to the first minutes, days and years of life can be gradually lost—or at least ignored and neglected—through a "culturally constructed forgetfulness" of adult societies.[15] Noted zoologist David Hay believes that the "adult world into which our children are inducted is more often than not destructive to their spirituality."[16] The divine flame may seem to burn out as we engage in a society and culture that seems to value the tangible over the intangible, the known over the unknown, and mastery over mystery.

Perhaps this is one idea that Jesus had in mind when he said we should have faith like little children (Mt 18:3). Perhaps he was speaking about the fact that children come into the world sensing the immediate and real presence of the living, transcendent God. But over time, as children learn from society that reason, science and logic alone offer "correct" insight about the universe, a closing off from feeling God's presence may evolve. The human and nonhuman subjects that we've been in relationship with gradually become objects for us to study from afar.

We're not saying that science and reason have no place in spirituality. But in many societies they're often held up over and against spirituality. For example, in the 2007 movie *Nacho Libre*, one of the main characters repeatedly says that he doesn't believe in God, he believes in science—as if belief in one cancels out belief in the other. But when objectivity, hard data and reason alone are touted as the only sources of truth, the relationship of intimacy and interaction becomes one of cold, hard facts and figures. Our drive to move beyond our here-and-now realities and explore the unknown can become one of memorization and regurgitation. Over time and without the warmth of intimate and personal encounters with God, the study of God can overshadow the authentic experience of God. This process can happen so gradually that we might not even perceive this change in ourselves and our children, this dimming of our spiritual capacities, this extinguishing of our spiritual flame. Fortunately, as many contemporary Christians are noticing their spiritual lights growing low, they're increasingly seeking out spiritual approaches to being Christian.

When Jesus called us to have faith like children, we believe that one thing that he was speaking about is opening ourselves to feeling God's transcendent presence once again, to seeing people, the world, God and ourselves as subjects rather than mere objects. In the words of Hay, "To maintain awareness of the here-and-now is to return to a kind of awareness found universally in infants."[17]

LEARNING TO KNOW ABOUT GOD

From our years of experience in children's ministry, we've seen our share of methods, approaches and resources that focus on helping children learn *about* God, faith, the Bible and the church. For example, the rotational model of children's ministry has become quite popular in the last few decades. For the length of a program, groups of children rotate from station to station where they learn about a common lesson or Bible story through games, arts and crafts, songs, storytelling and even snacks. No matter what station they find themselves at, they can learn the "point" of a particular Bible story; perhaps by decorating a Kleenex box at the craft station, which will remind children of how God comforted Paul during a storm and will surely comfort them.

These examples demonstrate a pervasive trend in ministry with children to help young people *know about God* while neglecting the imperative role they can play in helping them to *know* God, to have firsthand encounters with God. Faith becomes built on possessing the right understanding of God, the Bible, Jesus and so on, leaving little room (if any) for having faith-filled spiritual experiences of the living God.[18]

While learning specific sets of beliefs and practices are certainly crucial aspects of children's ministry and can help some children to know God, this can't be all that matters. When ministry with children becomes solely about learning what to believe and practice, children's spiritual capacities—their abilities to have intimate, personal connections with God—can get overshadowed and neglected. In the process young people might come to close themselves off from feeling God's presence in their everyday lives. Possessing information about God without having real encounters with the divine can lead to a faith that is overintellectualized and leaves no room for feeling. The warmth of God's personal touch is replaced by cold, hard facts about God.

Going further, children who equate the acquisition of knowledge with knowing God might struggle during the perils and challenges of life; when they yearn to sense the presence of God, the information they acquired at Sunday school might not sustain them. Knowing that God comforts us is certainly important, but it is no substitute for sensing God's comforting presence firsthand as one buries a goldfish, a grandparent or a friend.

And what about those times when God seems far away, when children don't sense the nearness of God's comforting presence? If all we have given children is a cognitive absolute that "God comforts us when we are sad," what will they think when they don't feel like this is true, when they don't sense the presence of the divine Comforter? While we certainly want to help them, such absolute views of God and faith can actually confuse children and damage their relationships with God.

LEARNING TO KNOW GOD

In the 2011 movie *The Way*, Martin Sheen portrays a sixty-something father who learned that his son died as he was beginning the Camino de Santiago, an 800-kilometer (500-mile) pilgrimage from Saint-Jean-Pied-de-Port, France, to Santiago de Compostela, Spain. Overcome with grief and encouraged by his son's desire, Sheen's character walks this journey by himself. Along the way he befriends three other pilgrims who make the trek with him, even though each one has set out on the pilgrimage for very different reasons.

The scenes and themes portrayed throughout *The Way* are abundantly rich in theological, spiritual and religious metaphor. As a whole the film depicts the human capacity for spirituality. Each of the four main characters comes from a different country and a vastly different walk of life. But they band together on pilgrimage. And we can do likewise with children. As John Westerhoff has said, "the child is a pilgrim, the adult is a pilgrim, and the spiritual journey is one of walking the road together."[19]

Parents, pastors, teachers and others who minister with young people can recognize that all children can encounter God, and these adults can seek to nurture these spiritual capacities of children. While there's certainly a place and time in children's ministry for helping youngsters fill their noggins with information about God, the Bible and Christianity, ministry with children helps the young to maintain relationships with God through which they sense God's presence in their lives. Rather than only offering lessons aimed at helping children learn about religious beliefs and practices, we can engage kids in practices through which they can know that they are in relationship with God. If, as we believe, children come into the world open to an immediate connection to God, our job becomes one of fostering this relationship, of fanning the divine flame inside each child, and helping young people maintain this openness as they grow.

As we nurture children in their relationships to God, as we walk the spiritual pilgrimage together, we can learn to give, to receive and to trust.

Giving of ourselves. We enter the world with a sense of felt connection to God. And as we grow, we attempt to make sense of and name this relationship. Hopefully, each one of us has felt the immediate and powerful presence of God as we moved through the different phases of life.

Children's ministry that kindles the divine spark in each child involves giving of ourselves as we share our stories and experiences with the children in our midst. When we speak of the presence of God in our lives, we empower children not only to seek out God in their own lives but provide them with words to express these ineffable spiritual experiences and allow them to have a safe place to speak about the power and presence of God in their own lives.

We are all spiritual creatures. Many of us have known times in our lives when we sense the immediate closeness of God. Why not open up and share these stories as gifts for the children in faith communities?

Receiving the wisdom of children. Although it is important for those of us who mentor, guide and lead children to share our testimonies of God's presence in our lives, it is equally important for us to open ourselves to receiving the wisdom that children offer to us as they share their stories and experiences of going beyond their present realities and sensing the company of God. After all, if we are all copilgrims who walk the spiritual journey together, then our fellow pilgrims who may be younger than us can guide us along the path.

We've already shown that children are inherently spiritual beings who are capable of feeling connected to God in real and life-changing ways. In recognizing this we can take the time to listen to them speak about these experiences, to hear them share with us about how they have known the immediate presence and power of God, and how it has affected their lives. And we can help them recognize and name the presence of God in their lives.

By doing so we respect the individuality of the child's experiences while affirming the power of the faith community. When children are welcomed into faith communities as members who legitimately contribute to the life of the church, we broaden our views of community to include those who are often marginalized because of their age. And we affirm and respect that each child brings his or her own unique gifts, perspectives and stories to the community.

But this respect must also flow to children who might not want to share about the times that they knew God was at hand, a here-and-now yet transcendent reality. At several points along the pilgrimage to Santiago de Compostela, Sheen's character refused to answer questions about his reasons and hopes for making the arduous journey across northern Spain. Since these reasons and hopes were so personal and so difficult to put into words, silence was often his answer.

For some people putting words to indescribable spiritual experiences makes these experiences lose something. As Rob Bell says, "The Christian Faith is mysterious to the core. It is about things and beings that ultimately can't be put into words. Language fails. And if we do definitively put God into words, we have at that very moment made God something God is not."[20] When some children are forced to speak about their spiritual experiences with God, they can be robbed of the very core of what made these experiences so special—the inexpressible and transcendent union with God. So as we encourage young people to share times when God has felt particularly close to them, let's do so gently, lovingly and respectfully. Let's invite children to share their lives and experiences with our faith communities without pressuring those who might wish to keep their encounters with God private. Invite, but don't insist.

On the other hand, there's more than one reason why some children might not talk about God experiences. Sometimes they remain silent about such experiences because they don't know that they have experienced God breaking into their lives or they don't have vocabulary to describe these experiences. (This isn't a problem that's exclusive to children.)[21] Teachers, pastors and parents may not have helped them learn to identify and speak about their transcendent experiences of God. In our zeal to make God and the Bible contemporary and child friendly, we can lose the use of transcendent and ephemeral language with children. We need to be intentional in watching the children we raise and work with for God experiences and point them out to them.

Trusting the Holy Spirit. Ultimately, children's ministry that focuses on the spiritual lives of children trusts in the power of the Holy Spirit to reveal God to young people. While we can certainly create spiritual environments and foster practices that can help children sense the presence of God, it is God alone, through the Spirit, who can reach out to them and let God's face shine upon them. When

God's Spirit touches our spirits, we can sense the immediate presence of God in our lives.

These Spirit-to-spirit connections have the power to keep children close to God for life. They keep the divine flame burning brightly within each child. With our faith and trust in the overwhelming power of the Holy Spirit, we can do all we can to help children sense God at work in their lives, to feel the immediate presence of the divine and to know through personal encounters with the living God that they are loved beyond all measures.

3

Formational Discipleship

We are disciples in training,
We're learning from the master,
We're on the road with Jesus,
Wherever he may lead.

We are disciples in training,
We're part of the adventure,
We're on this road together,
Let's see where it will lead.

BRYAN MOYER SUDERMAN, "Disciples-in-Training"

THROUGHOUT THE MANY YEARS THAT we've been involved in children's ministry, regardless of the location, denomination or capacity we were working in, we've heard parents, grandparents and other guardians express interest in ensuring that the ministries we were involved in were meeting their expectations. They've asked us countless questions about what we are doing to make sure that our involvement in children's ministry was helping their children learn the Bible, develop strong values and grow as Christians. We have appreciated the fact that parents and other caring adults were taking an interest in ensuring that their children's spiritual needs were being met.

During these conversations a few themes have popped up more frequently than others. One deals with learning, with gaining cognitive information about spiritual matters like the Bible, the church, God and salvation. "What do you do to make sure my kids understand that Jesus died for their sins?" "Why don't you do more memory verses?" "How do you ensure that my children are learning about the Bible?" These are just some of the many questions that we've been asked. And they seem to stem from an assumption that children's ministry ought to focus on helping children learn about spiritual and religious matters.

Another theme involves making sure that children's ministry is "age appropriate" and that it helps young people move through the proper stages of spiritual or faith development. Often these questions come from family members who are knowledgeable about one or more of the many theories of human development: Piaget's model of cognitive development, Fowler's stages of faith, Kohlberg's theory of moral development, to name just a few. "Is this children's ministry helping my child move from intuitive projective faith [Fowler's stage 1] to mythic-literal faith [Fowler's stage 2]?" "Are your lessons appropriate for the early preoperational thought of preschool children [Piaget's stage 2]?"

Other questions within this theme come from parents who might not have significant knowledge of human development, but believe that children ought to grow along a particular developmental trajectory. "Why has my son suddenly become obsessed with bugs and spends all of his time learning about spiders, mosquitoes and other insects?" "Why is my daughter always saying no to me when I ask her to do something?" "How come my eleven-year-old daughter changed from being 'Daddy's Girl' to being a recluse who hides away in her room talking to friends online instead of spending time with her family like she used to do?" A concern underlying these types of questions is whether their children are developing in healthy ways. It can be expressed in a simple and common question: Is this normal?

Both of these broad themes carry common assumptions about what parents and family members expect children's ministry will contribute to the life of their children. The first expects it to help children acquire information that is important for them to know. The second expects that ministry will help children pass through the appropriate stages of human development at the appropriate times in life. Yet both of them are based on presuppositions and assumptions that, while certainly important, shouldn't necessarily be the plumb line for how congregations, pastors and volunteers do ministry with children.

MORE THAN KNOWLEDGE ACQUISITION

Since Robert Raikes began educating youngsters in the slums of England in the latter part of the eighteenth century, Sunday school has been a staple of children's religious education and spiritual formation. Although its popularity has ebbed and flowed over the years, countless churches continue to rely on Sunday school (or offshoots like children's liturgy or children's church) as the primary means of offering young people Christian education as well as the main congregational activity for children.

While Sunday school certainly has done much to help children learn about many aspects of faith, the Bible and Christian living—to mention just a few—it often segregates children from the wider faith community. By dropping children off at Sunday school classrooms while the rest of the congregation gathers for worship, churches send implicit messages to children that what matters most about being Christian is learning the right things. As Gretchen Wolff Pritchard bluntly states, Sunday school tends to assume that "Adults come to church on Sunday in order to worship [and] children come to Sunday school to acquire information."[1]

Ministry with children that focuses solely on helping kids "learn the right things" tends to operate on the assumption that what matters most to the life of faith is one's ability to understand and articulate correct doctrine. In some circles a focus on the acquisition of knowledge is based on the belief that a proper theological knowledge of Christ's crucifixion is the key to salvation. No wonder so many churches build children's ministries that revolve around helping young people learn about Jesus' death.

Unfortunately, when children's ministry is based only (or largely) on these top-down assumptions and beliefs, the God-given agency, creativity, humanity and spirituality of children is undermined. Kids are seen as "safe" until a certain elusive age at which time they are suddenly at risk of eternal damnation if they don't pray the sinner's prayer or go through other theological hoops that are based on adult-centric views of faith and Christianity. Children's ministry is oriented around having young children learn the correct doctrines in the correct ways so that when they reach the "age of accountability," they can rest assured that their knowledge has saved them. Ivy knows of some churches that develop milestones for what a child should know and understand at certain ages. These theological plumb lines determine what is taught in education classes while children's progress is measured through quizzes and tests. John Wall notes that "Moral [we can add spiritual] capability is viewed on this model as something passively received from above."[2] Such views tend not to honor children's abilities to create their own ways of interpreting the world. They rob children of their God-ordained status as full and complete human beings, and they undermine their inherit spiritual capacities that they possess. While knowledge acquisition is definitely an important component of children's ministry, it ought not to be the sole or even primary purpose for it.

Additionally, these views often go hand-in-hand with assumptions about salvation that involve having children cross some invisible boundary from being separated from God to being united with God through their knowledge of salvation. If children are born already in connection with God, as we argued in chapter two, then helping them learn theological doctrines necessary to cross the bridge from damnation to salvation seems inappropriate. It can even seem like their inherent connection to God needs to be severed in order for children to freely choose God, when in fact God has already chosen them. Children's ministry ought to foster preexisting connections with God rather than a means for coaxing children across an invisible line of faith. It's about fanning the divine flame in each child rather than blowing it out and then encouraging kids to light it again.

MORE THAN DEVELOPMENT

The second set of questions outlined at the beginning of this chapter focus on issues of human development. Parents want to make sure that their children are where they should be (if not a little ahead) on theorized trajectories of psychological, moral, intellectual or spiritual development.

Modern psychology has provided us with incredible advances in understanding how human beings change and grow from birth to death. Many children's ministries, pastors and curriculum developers readily make use of theories of human development in their ministry with young people. Not only do they want to make sure that their ministries are age-and-stage appropriate, they also want to help move children along developmental paths to the next stages, periods and phases of human life.

While these efforts are commendable and have their merits, these developmental models of children's ministry, like the top-down knowledge acquisition models previously discussed, are also full of implicit assumptions about children and childhood that are problematic. First, even though developmental theories were proposed based on research in very particular contexts, they are presented as universal paths. There isn't much room for diversity along developmental trajectories outlined by theorists. Second, while they help us understand how children think, move, learn and even believe, they rob children of full humanity. John Wall is once again helpful in understanding this: "Childhood is interpreted through the lens of what children *are not yet*, namely, developed adults. . . . Adulthood, in contrast, is usually considered somehow complete, or at least more complete."[3] Children are seen more for what they ought to become rather than for what they are as children, and they're considered valuable for their future potential instead of the present being. Third, some developmental theories imply a sense that individualism and autonomy are fundamental to humanity, and they neglect and even rebuke notions of community and interdependence.

Although imperfect, theories of human development aid those who work with children (and people of any age) by offering lenses for making sense of different phases of the human journey. While they can be helpful, they shouldn't be the main basis of ministry with children (which is why we leave our discussion about how developmental theories are helpful to chapter eleven instead of using them as a basis for shaping how we do ministry with children). After all, David Fitch is correct that while psychology and human development may be helpful, they may also provide us with "interpretations of myself [and children] and ways of seeing the world that diverge dramatically from the ways of the gospel of Jesus Christ."[4] Jesus welcomed and affirmed people who were on very different paths of spiritual growth; theories of human development do not. Jesus said that children were exemplary members of the kingdom of God *as* children, and they don't need to grow up to be better people or better disciples; theories of human development do not. Jesus lived and taught an ethic and lifestyle of community and interdependence; theories of human development do not. We are, of course, making generalizations about developmental theories, which, as we said, are helpful. But as a whole they shouldn't be the foundation of children's ministry that is faithful to the way of Jesus.

SPIRITUAL FORMATION

While knowledge acquisition and human development theories can both contribute to a robust and vibrant children's ministry, neither one ought to be the focus. Using either as a foundation for ministry with young people falls short of kind of children's ministry that we are imagining in this book.

We believe that when children's ministry is first and foremost about spiritual formation. While it sometimes involves knowledge acquisition, spiritual formation is broader and deeper. Even though it can be buttressed by developmental theories, spiritual formation is more organic and child-honoring.

Spiritual formation affirms children as whole spiritual persons. They don't need to learn certain things or reach a certain developmental stage to be spiritual. They *are* spiritual. And, like people of all ages, their spiritual lives can be formed, nurtured and shaped. Spiritual formation is based on views of children that see them as inherently spiritual beings who are already in relationship with God. The idea of spiritual formation that we have in mind doesn't include a romanticized view of childhood that sees young children as perfect, sinless human beings who become marred by their experiences in the wider world. Nor does it hold to a view of children as little devils whose wills must be broken so they can know Christ and develop Christian values. Rather, it holds that children, like all of us, are disciples on a journey of spiritual formation.

Ellen Charry defines *formation* as "the nurturing of the soul that includes beliefs, values, attitudes, ideals, virtues, practices, and behavior through both formal and informal means."[5] Children's ministry that focuses on spiritual formation considers the factors that form children's spiritual lives as well as the ways in which a youngster's life can be shaped by these factors. Formation recognizes that children don't simply passively move along a universal developmental trajectory; context, culture, family, genetic code and communities all play a role in forming children's spiritual lives (and the spiritual lives of all people).

Moreover, spiritual formation acknowledges and respects the agency of childhood. Through the lens of spiritual formation, young people are active agents who creatively construct meaning and have a significant role in shaping their own spiritual lives. They don't simply pass through predetermined stages of growth, nor do they passively soak up information given to them, nor are their lives blindly constructed by the world around them. They are made in the image of God as creative agents who construct the world and are constructed by it, who form themselves and are formed by others. Spiritual formation moves from the perspective of adulthood to a view of growth in spirituality and faith from a child's perspective. It respects their humanity, creativity and agency.

Young disciples. Spiritual formation, in our view, is active, holistic, authentic, healthy, life-giving and hope-filled. But the reality of formation is that it is not always these things. Children's ministry focused on spiritual formation recognizes that young people can be formed in ways that are not very positive and don't contribute to their flourishing. Practical theologian Joyce Ann Mercer reminds us to be aware of the "possibility of children being negatively formed into distorted, oppressive, or otherwise problematic identities."[6] Children can be malformed.

The reality of church is that we who are part of the body of Christ are imperfect. Human sinfulness may not always be a popular topic, but it is real. And it shapes our faith communities. Local churches are imperfect communities of imperfect people. And as we who are part of churches attempt to form children, we need to remember that the communities, practices and ideas through which we attempt to shape the spiritual lives of young people are flawed. Mercer writes, "the faith identities in which children (and adults) are formed through participation in any particular church are at best provisional and partial. They stand in need of continual renegotiation and reformulation in light of continual learning and struggle in faith."[7] So we need to continually reconsider the faith and the faith communities through which we are forming young disciples. We need to be careful about how we go about forming children. We need to consider what we are forming kids into and how we help them form themselves.

Increasingly, we run into people who are uncomfortable calling themselves Christian. It's not that they don't believe in Jesus or that they are atheists. Their discomfort stems from so much evil and so many acts of hatred, violence and oppression in the world that have come from people who claim to be Christian, who perpetuate injustices while claiming such injustices to be the will of God.[8]

Refusing to calling oneself Christian has led to a trend of saying yes to terms like Christ follower and disciple of Jesus. This trend is not just recent. It's also ancient. In fact, the term *Christian* was given to early believers as a way of marking them as followers of Jesus. While we don't see the need to denounce ourselves as Christian people, we affirm that being Christian is essentially about being a disciple of Jesus.

John Westerhoff defines formation as "an intentional effort to engage in enculturalization, the natural process by which culture, a people's understandings and ways of life, their world view (perceptions of reality), and their ethos (values and ways of life) are transmitted from one generation to another."[9] He believes that such formation occurs through participation and practice of a community's way of life.[10] Christian spiritual formation, then, is about forming disciples of Jesus, people who participate in and practice the way of Jesus.[11] It helps people more closely follow in the path that he showed to us through his words and actions, and builds this journey into the core of their identities. Following Jesus is learn to walk in the way of Jesus one step at a time. It's about the journey—not the destination. Christians of every age are disciples, fellow pilgrims who walk the path together. Ryan Bolger and Eddie Gibbs have found that forward-thinking Christians tend to hold that the church "is made up of forgiven sinners, not perfected saints, who are at various stages of a life journey of discipleship."[12] Children can certainly be included in this view of church.

Children, like adults, can be followers of Jesus. There are no age restrictions on the path of discipleship. There isn't a cutout of Jesus holding his hand shoulder high with a speech bubble that reads, "You must be this high to follow me." And there are certainly no developmental restrictions either. No one needs to fill out a standardized test before embarking on the journey of discipleship.

When Jesus called his first disciples to him, he didn't tell them to study a book he wrote or work at getting to the next stage of development before following him. "As Jesus walked alongside the Galilee Sea, he saw two brothers, Simon, who is called Peter, and Andrew, throwing fishing nets into the sea, because they were fishermen. 'Come, follow me,' he said, 'and I'll show you how to fish for people'" (Mt 4:18-19). They left their nets behind and became apprentices to the Jesus way. They took their first steps on the journey of discipleship.[13]

The task of children's ministry, then, is to form young disciples, to help children build identities as followers of Jesus. It is about apprenticing children in the way of Jesus, the way of love, joy, reconciliation, peace, service, justice and mercy. It is about teaching, guiding and mentoring them about and through Jesus' words and actions. As Rob Bell has said, "The rabbi thinks we can be like him."[14]

Spiritual formation in this sense, then, is grounded in education. Or to be more precise it is grounded in pedagogy, a Greek-based word that Mary Elizabeth Moore states can be understood as *the act of leading people on a journey,* or leading across the earth. This involves walking with people, offering guidance when needed, and providing opportunities for people to discover new knowledge as they need it on their journey."[15] Clearly, this is more than acquiring knowledge or passing through developmental phases. It is a sacred journey.

Formation among friends. Children's ministry that emphasizes forming disciples of Jesus is about walking alongside children on the path of discipleship, apprenticing them into the way that Jesus laid out for all of us. We who work with children are disciples just like those young people in our midst. We are formed as disciples even as we form others. Children and adults walk the path together as equals on a common journey of discipleship.

But as disciples who may be more experienced in following Jesus, we have wisdom that can be passed on to the young disciples walking with us. So, even though we are children's equals and even though we are their friends along the journey, we can also be their guides along the path. Mike King's insight into youth ministry is also applicable to ministry with children: "Youth ministry is about being with youth, not just as a role model or friend but also as a spiritual guide and a traveling companion."[16]

Children's ministry can become a tale of friends on a spiritual journey, a journey of following Jesus one step at a time. As common pilgrims along this path, adults and children have much to teach one another. One of the problems with notions of childhood that emerged during the modern era is that they saw children as passive recipients of knowledge—sponges, blank slates, white paper, wet cement. But as the modern era fades and a new, postmodern era emerges, we can see children as pilgrims on a spiritual journey, pilgrims who walk alongside (not in front of or behind) adults.

Throughout our years of ministry with children, we have been blessed to make many young friends along the path of discipleship. The children in our lives have reminded us of the creativity, exuberance, authenticity and fear that come along with the journey. They show us what close connections to God look like. They remind us to thank God for the little things in life and that it's okay to cry out to God in gut-wrenching lament when we are overwhelmed, afraid or saddened. As we have followed Jesus side-by-side with young disciples, our spirits have been lifted and challenged, and we have been given the freedom to enjoy the journey. After all, children don't just walk along the path—they run, skip, slide, hop, play and dance as they follow in Jesus' footsteps.

As he reflected on the transition from modernity to postmodernity and what it might mean for the spiritual formation of children, John Westerhoff said,

> Modernity has provided us with many blessings, but it has also been detrimental to our spiritual lives. In this age of transition into a postmodern era with its new perceptions about human nature and life, it would be well for us to rethink our understandings of children so that we might nurture and nourish our spiritual lives by doing more with them and becoming more like them.[17]

Children's ministry in the way of Jesus focuses on children's spiritual formation, on helping young people become formed as disciples of Jesus. And as we who work with children seek to form them, we find ourselves formed in return by the young people in our midst. After all, we are all disciples in training. We walk a common path. We follow a common teacher. And we form as we are formed.

4

Vibrant Theologies

So human life is theology.
Virtually everything we do is inherently
theological. Almost every choice we make
reflects what we think about God.
There's no escaping it.

TONY JONES, *The New Christians*

◩ ◩ ◩

OUR SHELVES ARE LINED WITH BOOKS about children's ministry, books written to guide children's ministry leaders in developing a ministry that kids will want to show up for, that will keep them entertained and that will help them come to know God and develop a strong, lifelong faith.

Many of these books about helping children learn the Christian faith are undergirded with child psychology and human development theories that arose in the second half of the twentieth century. Sometimes the discussion about psychology is obvious and an author will, for example, include a chapter that introduces readers to Fowler's stages of faith development. But more often developmental theories remain implicit within the pages of these books. For example, countless books about children's ministry talk about the "age appropriateness" of their ideas. While they might not go into the nitty-gritty details about human development theories, an assumption behind these sorts of discussions is that children of different ages learn in different ways, that they go through processes of cognitive, moral, social and faith development as they grow up, and therefore they require different types of programs to meet their different developmentally appropriate needs.

Theories of human development and other ideas from the world of psychology are incredibly helpful for engaging in ministry with children. They give us glimpses into the hearts, minds and bodies of children, equipping us with insight about the youngsters in our churches, communities and homes. But one of the problems with so many children's ministry books is that they neglect to speak about children and children's ministry from a *theological* perspective. They talk about what a child is developmentally, psychologically, socially and even culturally, but they often forget to address theological notions of what it means to be a child. And since there is a trend in churches toward hiring children's pastors who have little (if any) theological education, children's ministry often operates without a vibrant understanding of theology—let alone an understanding of how children's ministry and theology intersect.

And this isn't unique to children's ministry. David Fitch argues that the church has given away its overall responsibility for spiritual formation to the theories, techniques and practices of modern therapy.[1] Psychology has come to dictate how we shape one another as Christian disciples, and he says this is problematic because "it is possible that psychology and Christianity may diametrically oppose one another."[2] While psychology can be a helpful tool (we'll address psychology and human development in chapter eleven), we can't forget that theology matters too!

In a basic sense theology is the study of the nature of God, religious belief and God's relation to the world. For thousands of years scholars have argued about what exactly Christian theology is and how we're to understand God's relation to the world particularly through the incarnation, ministry, death and resurrection of Jesus. John Westerhoff says that Christian theology "is a systematic reflection on every aspect of human life from the perspective of the Gospel."[3] And contemporary theologians are adding that theology also involves reflection on the gospel in light of human life. But theology isn't just for experts—all people think theologically.

In this chapter we take time to reflect on three ways theology intersects with children's ministry. First, we'll offer some words about theologies of childhood and explore, from theological perspectives, what it means to be a child, and how one's theological view of children will shape how one ministers with them. Second, we'll address ways that children are theologians, how they reflect and think theologically in ways that can be incredibly meaningful. And we'll round out the chapter by speaking about how the wider theological ethos of a church ought to affect how that church nurtures the spiritual life of its children. Of course, connections between theology and children are woven throughout the entire book. But by focusing squarely on theology, this chapter is meant to help us intentionally reflect on theological notions of childhood and come to understand why theology matters for children's ministry.

THEOLOGIES OF CHILDHOOD

Belief and ministry are mutually shaped. What we believe about God, humanity, the world and following Jesus has a hand in shaping how we think ministry should be done. And our experiences in the world also shape what we think of it. So belief affects action, and action affects belief.

But a quick Google search for "theology, children's ministry" shows that this relationship between theology and ministry—between what we believe about children and how we minister with them—is often overlooked. The first few pages of search results might include some research about children's ministry in mainline churches, posts and articles about teaching theology and doctrine to children, and websites of seminaries and colleges touting their children's ministry programs. But what doesn't make it to the search results are articles or websites that address the theological basis for children's ministry in churches. But this doesn't mean that theology is absent. It doesn't mean that no one throughout all of history stopped to ask theological questions about what it means to be a child and to nurture the spiritual lives of children.

While they haven't often devoted specific writings to theology and children, church leaders and theologians throughout history have given thought to children, Jesus' response to them and what they mean to the life of the church. But there hasn't been a consensus about theological meanings of childhood.

Marcia Bunge has been at the forefront of the movement to explore theologies of childhood. She's sifted and sorted through different ways that "the child" has been analyzed by theologians throughout history and has concluded that there are at least six broad theological perspectives.[4]

Gifts of God, sources of joy. The gift of God perspective sees children as divine gifts that are bestowed by God upon families and communities. This is a view prevalent in the Old Testament, where several passages speak about the joy that comes from having children (Ps 127:3-5; 128:1-4) and consequently the sorrow of not being able to procreate (1 Sam 1). And the Jewish culture of Jesus' time shared this view of children as divine gifts, as signs of God's blessing on the family and the entire community.

Such a view can romanticize children as little angels in need of protection, but at its core it offers a radical message. Bunge notes that "Viewing children as gifts of God to the whole community radically challenges common assumptions of them as property of parents, as consumers, or as economic burdens to the community."[5] Children, as divine gifts, are to be cherished, valued and protected.

Sinful creatures, moral agents. But not all theological views are so lovely. Christian theologians throughout history have seen children as sinful beings and little devils. Based on interpretations of many biblical texts (Gen 8:21; Ps 58:3; Prov 22:15; Rom 3:9-10), church leaders like John Calvin, Jonathan Edwards and James Dobson have focused on children as inheritors of original sin, which is to be purged from the child through instruction in the right way to live. In this view the parental task is to suppress and control the child's natural depravity.

This perspective has often led to misguided and warped understandings of children that support abuse in order to cast out the evil within them. Tempted as we may be to throw out this view, Bunge warns us not to do so. After all, it can help correct an extreme view of children as innocent beings who lack moral agency. In fact, seeing children as sinful means that they must be moral agents; they must be human beings who make moral choices. New England pastor and theologian Jonathan Edwards not only assumed that children were sinful creatures but also that they had "real minds and souls quite capable of dealing with deep existential worries and able to receive grace."[6] So while it may be easy to simply throw this perspective away, it calls attention to the fact that children are accountable and autonomous moral agents.

Developing beings in need of guidance and instruction. A third perspective that's surfaced in Christian tradition is that of children as beings in a state of development who require instruction, guidance and nurture in order to properly develop. Several commonly cited biblical passages about instruction have formed out of and fed into this perspective, including Proverbs 22:6 ("train children in the way they should go") and Ephesians 6:4 ("raise [children] with discipline and instruction about the Lord").

This view is also seen in the writings of theologians who address the importance of children's spiritual formation. Early church theologian John Chrysostom wrote about the role of the church with both children and parents, emphasizing "the need for socialization of the young into the church, and the powerful unitive and communicative love that the parent-child nexus infuses into human society."[7] He used the metaphor of parents as artists to explain the spiritual vocation of parenthood. During the Protestant Reformation both Luther and Calvin created materials for parents to help them in the religious education of their children, demonstrating the importance of the proper development of these little creatures, as did Horace Bushnell in the nineteenth century.

While there is much to praise in this view, it can lead us to see children as not-yet adults. It underlines what children are *not* and encourages adults to do all they can to help children successfully pass through childhood and into adulthood, a time when life is seen to really matter.

Fully human, made in God's image. This view highlights the full humanity of children, so it provides a helpful counterpoint to the view of children as developing creatures. Because they're fully human, they are worthy of respect, dignity and human rights. Drawing from Genesis 1:27, this perspective claims that as full human beings, children are made in the image of God and have inherent value as such. This wasn't a common notion during Jesus' day. In ancient Greco-Roman society, children were sometimes seen on par with animals—quite a far throw from fully human image-bearers.

But theologians have championed this view throughout history. Bunge notes that third-century theologian Cyprian argued that all people—regardless of age, ability or character—are equal to one another because they are made in God's image. And just last century Catholic theologian Karl Rahner (who penned a treatise called "Ideas for a Theology of Childhood") argued that children's full humanity means that they are deserving of respect and dignity.[8]

Models of faith, sources of revelation. New Testament scholar Judith Gundry writes about both Jesus' view of children and the views of his surrounding culture.[9] Then, as now, society tended to hold ambivalent notions of childhood. While ancient Greco-Roman culture did not always place great esteem in childhood for childhood's sake, parents did find value in children and took pleasure in them. Nevertheless, the immature state of a child was not something to be desired but, instead, something to outgrow. They saw childhood as simply a training ground for adult life. But Jesus taught his followers that they should enter the reign of God "as a child," a seemingly simple assertion that has received all sorts of interpretations.

Jesus' radical words are a shining example of this fifth perspective of childhood, which sees youngsters as models of faith and sources of revelation. While other conceptions hold that children are in need of instruction, this view affirms that children have much to teach us. In Bunge's words, "They can prophesy and praise God. They can be vehicles of revelation, models of faith, and even paradigms for entering the reign of God."[10] This perspective has been overlooked throughout much of history, with the scales tipped by theologians writing about teaching children rather than those writing about learning from them. But Bunge holds up Friedrich Schleiermacher as an example of a theologian who highlighted children as sources of revelation and models of faith. He found much to learn about faith through a childlike spirit and was careful not to boil down Jesus' mandate to enter the reign of God as a child to one ideal or another.

Orphans, strangers and neighbors in need of compassion and justice. The final perspective that Bunge articulates is that of children as orphans, neighbors and strangers who need justice and compassion in their lives. The Bible, and Christian history, is replete with stories about children (many of whom are unnamed) who suffer as victims and are in need of help.

Although Christian theology has sometimes been used to harm and victimize the least of these, there are shining examples of theologians who worked to bring justice and offer compassion to suffering children. While Chrysostom wrote about children's spiritual formation, he related it to Jesus' command to love one's neighbor. Children should be included in understanding who "my neighbor" is. John Wesley began several institutions to help care for poor and oppressed children, and Pamela Couture's research shows that many who carry on Wesley's legacy in the Methodist church continue to offer compassion and work for justice in the lives of children.[11] Concern for suffering children is not a recent phenomenon for church communities and the people who think or write about them.

Tension. During his presentation at the 2012 Children, Youth, and a New Kind of Christianity conference, John Westerhoff offered a compelling definition of heresy and truth.[12] Heresy, he said, is failing to keep two diametrically opposing views in tension. For example, Jesus is fully human and fully divine—moving to one extreme or the other causes people to get caught in heresy. Truth is in the tension.

This view is congruent with many churches that are journeying together in expanding and enlivening Christianity in our world. After centuries of extremism in one form or another, several people (in the church and beyond) have grown cautious and skeptical of those who hold to a particular exclusionary and extreme view. More people are beginning to seek out middle ground, third ways and balance between opposing poles. For example, several people are avoiding partisan political views that favor either the left or the right (which may be either

blue or red, depending on the country), opting instead for a "purple"
perspective, one that remains cautiously critical of either strong blue or
red political views and combining the best of both worlds. These third
ways and middle grounds aren't simply redefinitions of old paradigms —
they lead us to discover new paradigms.

Bunge has come to similar a conclusion in her understanding of
children and childhood. She argues that "When incorporated into
Christian theologies of childhood and held in appropriate balance and
tension, these six perspectives have tremendous implications for com-
bating simplistic and destructive conceptions of children and strength-
ening the commitment to them within Christian communities."[13] She
goes on to say that holding these six perspectives in tension helps religious education initiatives honor children's questions while helping
cultivate their growing spiritual capacities. It calls the church to care
for all children, since each one bears the image of God, and to become
advocates for children at home and across the globe.

And she doesn't live in this tension alone. Scholars like John Wall,
Bonnie Miller-McLemore and Joyce Mercer all advocate for holding
different and opposing theological views of children in tension. For
example, after offering observations about perspectives of children as
inherently pure and inherently sinful, Miller-McLemore says that
neither view is without its problems: "The reign of the cherished, romanticized child created its own set of problems every bit as troubling
as belief in the sinful, corrupt child had done."[14]

And it's not only contemporary theologians who live within the
tension of different theological perspectives of childhood. In his research into children in the theology of sixteenth-century Anabaptist
leader Menno Simons, Keith Graeber Miller argues that Simons believed in the "complex innocence" of childhood.[15]

Keeping these theological perspectives of children in tension reminds us that, like all other theological assertions, our ideas are limited
and partial at best. A growing number of people are recognizing the
limits of human knowledge. More people are realizing that all human
understanding is partial at best. When we hold these different theological perspectives of childhood in tension, we guard ourselves from

moving too far into one camp and fooling ourselves into thinking that we've cornered the market on truth. And we respect the fullness and complexity of children.

Children's ministry needs to seriously consider theological views of children and develop a robust understanding that lives within a tension of perspectives we've outlined in this chapter. Moving too far in one direction or another leads to unhelpful and even downright harmful practices. And when we do ministry within this tension, it may mean that some practices need to be questioned and unlearned. For example, focusing only on children as sinful creatures tends to lead to practices of conversionism that leave little if any room for more gradual formation. But another perspective—children as developing beings—can lend itself to ministry with a sole purpose of helping children gradually grow in their faith and can ignore those mountaintop experiences that form faith in more dramatic ways. Maintaining a theology in tension can allow ministry to become not either-or but both-and as churches encourage ongoing formation in children while pausing to celebrate moments in which a child's faith undergoes more climactic change. Children's ministry in the way of Jesus recognizes that truth is in the tension.

FROM THE MOUTHS OF BABES

Clearly, it's not unheard of to think about children and children's spiritual formation theologically. Jesus talked about children and used them as a metaphor for gaining entrance into the kingdom of God. Early church fathers were interested in theological understandings of children and parenting. Later influential Christian theologians wrote about children, their place in the church and the meaning of their baptism. And contemporary theologians are uncovering new ways of thinking theologically about children and children's spiritual formation. Throughout these conversations pastors have chimed in as well, correcting, nuancing and challenging theologians through their perspectives as people with feet on the ground in local churches.

This calls attention to the circular nature of theological understanding. How we understand God and God's relationship with us doesn't just come down to us from scholars and thinkers through the ages. What we do in our local faith communities informs broader theological understanding. The theological process is not top-down but circular, not hierarchical but communal. We believe certain things about God and the world, and these beliefs should inform how we live and act in our faith communities. But as we live out our lives and try to live in the way of Jesus in our churches we can come to a better understanding of God and the world expanding our theological understanding.

Last summer Ivy had a discussion with a group of nine- and ten-year-olds who live in New York City, more specifically Manhattan. They were talking about Jesus' parable of the man who gave a party and invited all of his wealthy friends. None of them were able to attend because they all had other things to do. So the man sent his servants out to invite the poor, the sick and the shunned to the party.

This is a classic parabolic description of the kingdom of God. So Ivy expected these children to follow the party line and talk about how the man's friends had really blown it by giving up this wonderful, once-in-a-lifetime party for things they could have done on almost any other day. Instead, the children put the blame on the man who gave the party. They said he should have given his guests more notice—after all, they had busy schedules and shouldn't have been expected to just drop everything to go to this man's party. Still unwilling to let go of her interpretation of the parable, Ivy tried to explain how the party was the best party that had ever been given—so spectacular that no one would want to miss it, no matter what! These kids still weren't buying it. The man's friends had their own schedules to keep and should not be expected to give those up for anything.

While we weren't able to come to a consensus about our interpretations of this parable (and surely there are many interpretations), it's clear that these kids were doing theology. More specifically, they were engaging in theological interpretation about the character of the kingdom of God. And in the process, Ivy's own theology of the communal work of Scripture interpretation was at work that morning, reminding her that children don't just learn the theologies that we teach them—they too are theologians, making meaning and interpreting God's work in the world for themselves.

Their interpretation of this parable was very different from any interpretation Ivy had ever encountered, but it certainly was informed by the daily lives and worldviews of the young people doing the interpreting. And we think their interpretation adds to more common understandings of this particular parable. Just hearing what children who sporadically attend church have to say about a parable adds to our contemporary understanding of what this parable has to say to us, expanding our theological outlook and understanding. Churches can indeed listen to young theologians and add their fresh understandings to the theological canon.

Based on what we believe about children and spirituality—that each child is born with an inherent spiritual capacity—seeing children as theologians doesn't come out of nowhere. Children have experiences of God. They know God. So why would we assume that they are only passive consumers of theology and not active producers of it? In reality, children impart theological wisdom in at least two ways.

Children as theologians. First, their ideas and imaginations allow them to understand their experiences of God in unique ways. In fact, one could argue that children should be some of our church's main theologians-in-residence, since their understandings of their God experiences are less likely to be fettered and boxed in by the adult conceptions that we teach them as they grow up. Their experiences are often more raw and uncensored, and they are open to more creative and imaginative insight.

But sadly we've witnessed countless instances when adults fail to give children the respect they deserve as theologians in their own right. (And we admit that we haven't always taken the time to really listen to the wisdom that children share with us.) In fact, Dave witnessed it as we were writing this chapter. When catching up on his Facebook news, a friend posted a very insightful comment that her five-year-old daughter made. It wasn't just *very* insightful—it was *incredibly* insightful. It blew Dave's mind and made him look at things in new ways.

But while Dave's friend seemed to share his awe at this young girl's ideas, her Facebook friends diminished its value by playing up the cutesiness of it. Comments included "So precious," "cute," and "That's AWESOME!!! Hahahaha!!! :)" Of course, these aren't really negative comments. But they seem to rob this girl's ideas of their power, making them just the cute and whimsical comments of a young, naive child.

In recent decades Christians in all sorts of traditions have been exploring new ways of doing theology. For many this means paying close attention to theological voices that have traditionally been marginalized. Pastors, educators and laypeople are finding fresh theological insights in the voices of people who have typically been ignored by mainstream (white, male, straight, able-bodied, Western) theology. Children are certainly one of these marginalized groups. They have spoken, but we've often ignored (or even silenced) them.

Churches are also playing with how to do theology in community. The days when the learned theological expert imparts wisdom to the congregation are over. Faith communities like Church of the Apostles in Seattle, Washington, and Emmaus Way in Durham, North Carolina, attempt to do life in community—and this means doing theology in community.[16] And since children ought to be valued as contributing members of our faith communities, they are our fellow theologians who share, collaborate and at times butt heads with us as we wrestle with theology together.

Being open to insight gleaned from the theological views of children is consistent with the view of children we put forward in this book. If we're all pilgrims on a spiritual journey, then we need to remember this when we get into conversations with children. We need to remember that they too know God. And we need to remember Jesus' words: "I praise you, Father, Lord of heaven and earth, because you have hidden these things from the wise and learned, and revealed them to little children" (Mt 11:25 TNIV).

Revealing God. But children not only reveal theological insights by sharing their ideas with us. As full human beings made in the image of God, they reveal insights about God that are often more difficult to see (or easier to suppress and ignore) in adults. Church services can often be planned in ways that allow for extended periods of uninterrupted contemplation in an orderly environment. And many people easily equate spiritual practices with quiet, calmness and stillness.

Children, on the other hand, aren't always orderly, quiet, calm or still. They can be loud, messy, rambunctious, bothersome and unpredictable—all qualities on the opposite side of the spectrum from what people tend to think of when they imagine time spent with God. But an honest look at God as God appears in the Bible will show that God too can demonstrate these attributes. True, God can be heard in stillness and silence (1 Kings 19:12), but God can be known to make a mess (Gen 7), to be noisy and loud (Deut 5:22; Rev 21:3), and to interrupt the orderliness of people's lives (Ex 4–5; Acts 9:1-31). Bonnie Miller-McLemore reminds us that when we see God in the chaos that can seem to follow children wherever they go,

> God is no longer an all-powerful, unchanging Lord in the sky. Instead we glimpse a more puzzling, raging, weeping, shouting, pleading, disruptive, disturbing, and even evolving God, moving within the deep, appearing in unexpected and unplanned places, and sometimes even coming to us as the "Discomfortor" as well as the Comforter.[17]

So maybe children are more like God than we often assume.

For many people this is a radical idea. A few years ago Dave wrote an article for a Christian magazine and said that children, as bearers of the *imago Dei*, reveal less-pleasing images of God (at least less-pleasing to adult sensibilities and standards). Shortly after the issue of the magazine came out, the editors received this note from a reader: "I just saw your article on children in the church. The intro to the article talks about kids teaching us that God is 'playful, loud, messy and unpredictable.' Since when do we learn about the attributes of God through observation of the behavior of children? This is completely unscriptural."[18]

Clearly, this reader felt as though Dave's comments went against the faith that she or he holds dear. To this day Dave's still not sure why this idea rubbed this reader the wrong way. But he's thankful that the magazine's editor stood behind him while inviting the reader to share her or his frustration in an official letter to the editor.

But not everyone objects to the idea that children reveal insights about God. We've heard of one church that has actually transformed its responses to the fussing and crying of young children during worship services. Instead of the typical response of "get that child out of here so we can worship in peace," the congregation uses this noise "as a signal to pray for those in our world who are in need or cannot care for themselves."[19] May we all humble ourselves to receive the wisdom that children reveal to us simply through their presence.

CREATING A FORMATIONAL ENVIRONMENT: IT'S ABOUT THE THEOLOGY

How we think of children theologically should influence the way we minister with them. The authors of *Children Matter* say that "the church's view of God and his people affects the way its members relate to and interact with each other as well as the ministry practices they develop."[20] For example, several theologically conservative denominations and churches believe that in order to enter into God's kingdom, a person must have a conversion experience in which he or she turns from sinful ways and accepts the way of Jesus. Therefore, these types of churches often put great emphasis in their children's ministries on bringing children toward a "born again" experience through teaching and other activities. A common central tenet of their children's ministries springs from this foundational theological concept and the particular understanding of salvation that they hold true.

Churches that don't understand the concept of salvation in quite the same way tend not to put this kind of emphasis on what has been termed a "crisis conversion" experience, and they usually do children's ministry in fundamentally different ways. Some churches focus on sanctification rather than salvation, and they help children grow into the salvation that was bestowed on them when they were baptized as infants. Others try to find a balance between dramatic experiences of conversion and a gradual lifelong process of spiritual formation.

However, this adherence to living out a particular theological tenet is not always found throughout a church's children's ministry, and sometimes congregations do ministry in ways that contradict their theological beliefs and central faith practices. For example, for a time Ivy traveled around the American Midwest selling Sunday school and vacation

Bible school curriculum to congregations. Her territory included quite a few mainline churches. While these churches were often a hard sell when it came to Sunday school curriculum, they were eager to purchase the VBS curriculum because they enjoyed its themes and the activities it provided for kids. However, this particular curriculum was heavy on the salvation/conversion message, but most of the mainline churches on her circuit placed an emphasis on the salvation that a child inherits at baptism and into which the child gradually grows. Practical theologian Joyce Mercer attests to the fact that Ivy's not the only one who witnessed this phenomenon, arguing that it "contributes to a situation in which mainline faith communities may adopt theological perspectives and religious practices in relation to children that do not particularly fit with the rest of their theology and mission."[21]

One day, as Ivy was discussing this disconnect with a Lutheran pastor in charge of children's education, the pastor simply said, "Oh, we just gloss over those parts." Fun activities and an enticing theme trumped theology for this church.

We've already spoken about how theological views shape our ministry with children. And we've shown that children are young theologians who actively construct religious and spiritual meaning of their lives and experiences. Here we take these discussions further by arguing that children's ministry (like any particular congregational ministry) should be treated as a microcosm of the wider formational ethos of a church. This means that how we minister with children needs to be congruent with our wider community and faith tradition.

This has been an ongoing challenge in churches thinking about new ways of doing ministry and being the church. The rising tide of change sweeping over the church has far too often been preoccupied with forming faith in adults and, to a lesser extent, teenagers. Ministry with children has, in our view, often operated through off-the-shelf curricula that don't seem to appropriately reflect the emerging ethos of the wider faith community. So while all sorts of innovative approaches for ministry with adults have been forged, children have often been left out and left behind. This is not to say these churches don't care about their children. They do! But perhaps frozen with fear or simply predisposed to focus on adults, many churches enculturate children into theological ideas and practices that the wider community has come to question and even reject. We've heard all sorts of leaders lament the fact that their ministries with children pass on beliefs, values and practices that many of the adults in their church—including their pastors, teachers and parents—found they had to unlearn on their journey of walking in the way of Jesus. It goes without saying that those responsible for children's spiritual formation need to end this cycle. And it ends as children's ministry becomes congruent with the wider formational endeavors of the faith community.

But how often do those of us in children's ministry actually take a step back and evaluate whether our work in children's spiritual formation appropriately lines up with the wider church's formational endeavors? We might steer away from certain publishers or materials because in our circles these have been labeled "liberal" or they seem "close-minded." Or we might try to infuse children's ministry with certain characteristics, such as particular times for contemplative prayer or specific opportunities for kids to accept Jesus. However, too often the criteria for shaping ministry and selecting resources tend to be the latest craze, the latest successful model that has seen growth in numbers, the curriculum that promises a care-free VBS, and the program the megachurch across town is running.

Children's ministry in the way of Jesus rests firmly within the wider formational and ministerial activities of faith communities and traditions. How do churches make sure this is the case? How do they form their children's ministry in ways that are intertwined with the wider community? And how can children's ministry shape and reshape the practices and beliefs of the wider congregation?

A first step is to take inventory of the formation practices and assumptions of a faith community and faith tradition. Of course, we have argued that the ultimate goal of Christian spiritual formation is to help people walk in the way of Jesus, to be disciples of the risen Christ. But the call to discipleship is contextual. Those aspects of discipleship that are emphasized will shift from church to church and tradition to tradition, as will our formational efforts. While some congregations focus on helping people have firsthand experiences of God through contemplative spiritual practices like *lectio divina* and centering prayer, others place more weight on helping people be the hands and feet of Jesus by working for justice. By taking inventory of these assumptions within the wider church or denomination, we who minister with children take crucial first steps in ensuring that our efforts are theologically congruent with those of the larger community of faith.

Next, a congregation can reflect on forming (or reforming) the purpose of its children's ministry in light of the results of its inventory and the greater goal of forming disciples. Is the reason for ministry with children to make sure kids make conscious, marked decisions to follow Jesus? Is it to take seriously the faith community's baptism or dedication vows of enfolding children into the Christian faith? Is it because the church desires to minister to, for and with children, supporting their spiritual nurture and formation? These are all worthy purposes—and there are countless others. When we ask these questions, we take important steps in enfolding children's ministry into the wider ethos, theologies and contexts of our congregations and faith traditions.

We're not saying churches ought to avoid everything that seems to go against their theological beliefs and practices. But we've seen too many folks uncritically use resources that are theologically inappropriate for their contexts—a significant problem for churches that are reimagining faith and formation in contemporary contexts. Since there aren't many resources available to help these churches pass on their faith to children, many leaders and teachers resort to using curricula that teach things that the church, their teachers and the children's parents don't hold true. Does this set children up to form a faith infected with inconsistencies and contradiction? Only time will tell.

Context matters. The theological assumptions of churches, denominations and Christian traditions matter to the way we do children's ministry. Recognizing the contextual nature of life is central to an emerging view of the world. Colonialism has shown us the dangers (we can even say evils) of imposing ways of living in one context onto people in other contexts. We who seek to nurture the spiritual lives of children need to be careful not to buy into the mentality that what works best in one context ought to be duplicated a thousand times over in other contexts. We need to seek out "glocalized" ways of doing ministry, ways that critically assess and adapt broader global trends in manners consistent and appropriate for our local contexts. And we need to keep asking ourselves if the faith we are sharing with children is really a faith we value for ourselves.

BEYOND GIMMICKS

The Broadway musical *Gypsy* includes a song titled "You Gotta Get a Gimmick." "You gotta get a gimmick if you wanna get ahead," the lyrics read. It seems like the last few decades of children's ministry have been centered on who has the best gimmick to attract people to their churches rather than thinking carefully how to best minister with the children in their midst. We've known several faith communities that have based their children's ministry initiatives on providing a fun environment and ease for volunteer teachers rather than looking closely at what they really believe about the nature of God, the church and children, and how this translates into the whys, hows and whats of children's ministry. And we've seen all sorts of churches ignore or "cutesify" new insights children bring to the theological landscape, instead only focusing on making sure children believe the right things. But it hasn't always been this way. And it doesn't need to continue being this way.

There is great potential for those of us who seek fresh approaches to ministry with children to chart paths forward. We can understand that children's ministry done with consistency and integrity means that what churches, pastors, teachers and parents believe theologically will influence every node of our children's ministries. And we can admit that children's ministry doesn't merely teach children the "correct" doctrine, but also listens to the theological insights that children offer as they discover for themselves what it means to be Christian, to love God and to live as disciples in the way of Jesus. And we can continually work to make sure that wider theological beliefs and practices of our congregations and traditions shape our ministry with children, who also shape and reshape these churches and traditions.

5

Living Stories

Take it. It's yours. Do with it what you will.
Tell it to your children. Turn it into a play. Forget it.
But don't say in the years to come that you would have lived
your life differently if only you had heard this story.
You've heard it now.

THOMAS KING, *The Truth About Stories*

◻ ◻ ◻

IN HIS 2003 MASSEY LECTURES, Thomas King began by stating that "the truth about stories is that that's all we are."[1] Human beings live and die by their stories. We are a storied people. And the stories we tell and hear are more than simply entertainment; they have the power to form and transform who we believe ourselves to be and what we believe we are called to do. The tales we recount shape the core of who we are and act as lenses through which we see and live in the world.

Phyllis Tickle has written that communities hold to stories that represent "the shared history—mythic, actual, and assumed—of the social unit."[2] She likens a community's stories to waterproof coverings that protect the inside of a cable (which is made up of a community's spiritual, moral and corporal life as well as its common imagination) from forces on the outside. The cover makes sure that the insides of the cable remain intact. In a similar way, stories form a protective barrier around what we hold to be true, sacred or meaningful in the world.

They affect how we see the world, how we interact with those around us, what we value and every other part of our lives. We are our stories.

Human beings begin hearing and learning stories from an early age. Through enculturation in communities and cultures, we pick up on cues about the stories that are sacred to these contexts. Whether or not we actually sit down to tell them a tale, the children in our lives are gaining insight into the stories we live by.

Unfortunately, the stories that young people hear and see are not always positive, challenging and life-giving. Sometimes they are hateful, dark and sinister narratives that teach young people to fear the unknown and to put up walls to keep out those who are different. As King has written, "Stories are wondrous things. And they are dangerous. . . . So you have to be careful with the stories you tell. And you have to watch out for the stories that you are told."[3]

In the Region of Waterloo, in southwestern Ontario, there's a picturesque tower that stands along the banks of the winding Grand River. Named the Waterloo Pioneers Memorial Tower, this designated national historic site of Canada marks the arrival of German Mennonites who made their way north from Pennsylvania and settled in the area. It commemorates the bravery, ingenuity and hard work of these pioneers and their early contributions to this region of the country. The historic plaque and educational signs at the tower tell a story of heroism, of new beginnings, of Christian sacrifice and dedication.

But, as King reminds us, we must be careful of the stories we are told. The dominant stories—those that clamor the loudest for our attention and allegiance—are usually written by winners. But there are other stories—those kept alive by the memories of those who lost, who were captured, oppressed, marginalized and murdered. The story of pioneering determination told by the Waterloo Pioneers Memorial Tower omits and overshadows the story of exile, oppression and broken promises made to those who had been living on the land—the people now known as the Six Nations. Their stories are not commemorated by the tower. They are swept under the rug of national pride and government initiatives. But this does not mean that their stories are not real.

GOD'S STORY

Contrary to popular practice, the Bible is not a storehouse of propositional truth about God or even a legal constitution that lays out the rules for proper living. It's a storybook, a community library of stories about God and God's interactions with humanity.[4] While there are certainly letters, poems and songs contained within its pages, the great majority of the Bible contains stories. And like episodes of a good television series that tell smaller pieces of the larger story, so the books, chapters and verses of the Bible offer a piece of the larger story of God.

Too often children's ministry offers young people different age-appropriate episodes of God's story without helping them make sense of it as a coherent whole. When offered as stand-alone stories, the Bible can easily become a rigid reference for how to live a Christian life, with each story bringing a moral or a point. (We'll talk more about this in chapter six.) Ivy has called this the "Aesop-fableization" of the Bible. And even though this choppy rerun-based approach to teaching the Bible might help children learn to obey their parents, to share their toys and to know that Jesus died for their sins, these lessons and morals remain shallow and disconnected from one another.

When the Bible is offered to children as the overarching story of God's interactions with humanity—one that includes many different episodes—these shorter lessons and points are infused with larger meaning and truth. Children can learn that obeying their parents isn't as simple as it sounds, for God is their divine parent, as well as their parents' divine parent, so they ought to honor their parents *and* God, and struggle with what to do when honoring one means going against the guidance of the other. Learning to share one's toys becomes part of the overarching theme of love that is woven throughout God's story—love not only for the neighbor but also for the stranger and for enemies. And Jesus' death is understood in more complex and nuanced ways—as the result of threats to the status quo, the attempted triumph of violence over peace and God's ultimate love for humanity.

Exploring the Bible in this way requires a broader notion of truth. Truth involves more than just whether a piece of writing is fiction or nonfiction, whether the events in the Bible actually happened or not.

Truth is in how a story speaks to our human condition and how it works to transform us. This type of truth exists in the episodes that make up the grand epic of God's story.

Clearly, teaching the Bible as an overarching story of God is more difficult than teaching it as a collection of smaller, disjointed stories. Teaching children the complex, abstract ideas embedded in the larger narrative may seem like an impossible task. After all, social scientists over the past several decades have shown that young children's minds tend to be geared toward the concrete. And in some cases it may actually be developmentally inappropriate to try to teach children (especially younger children) God's epic narrative. But this doesn't mean that we can't lay a foundation by helping them come to know different parts of the story, always seeking to make connections and fit the larger narrative together when appropriate to do so.

So how do we offer the Bible as God's story without overwhelming children, parents, teachers and ourselves?

A PUZZLING WAY OF TEACHING

A simple answer might be to teach the Bible linearly, to begin at Genesis 1 and end at Revelation 22, telling the story bit by bit over a number of years. But there are other ways of teaching the Bible that allow us to share the epic story of God with children in gradual ways.

One way is to help children get to know God's story as they might get to know a friend. When two or more people start developing a friendship, they often begin by sharing stories surrounding their present lives and perhaps some stories from the past that are relevant to these present stories or to things that the new friends hold in common. As the friendship deepens, they might share other stories from their lives—but not usually in chronological order. Even though their life stories are told to one another out of chronological order, rather than confusing one another, the telling and hearing of these stories allows these friends become closer and more intimate.

This is one way of understanding how we tell God's story to children. Another analogy that we've found helpful is to think of teaching God's story like putting together a puzzle.

When we tear the seal on a new puzzle and pour hundreds of pieces (or thousands, if we're ambitious) onto the table, it can be difficult to know where to begin. Often, it's the pieces that are part of the subject of the picture that tend to jump out at first. After all, the main subject of the painting or photograph is usually in the foreground and contains the most important details.

Let's say, for example, that the puzzle is a photograph of the front of Notre Dame Cathedral in Paris against a clear, blue sky. It wouldn't make sense to begin with the sky, aimlessly placing random pieces of blue together to see if they fit. A good place to start would be to collect the most important pieces of the puzzle—those that stand out—and place them together until the cathedral's famous rose window or the north and south bell towers are assembled. Then it might be helpful to move on to the doors and the other features of the building until the entire façade of the cathedral is assembled. At this point, the central image of the puzzle would be in one piece. Regarding the sea of blue pieces on the table, it might make sense to collect all of the pieces of sky that form the border of the puzzle and, once the border is assembled, gradually put the rest together until every piece is where it belongs.

In a similar way, teaching the Bible involves piecing together the stories of the Bible in a way that gradually makes the larger story of God come together in clear focus. It makes sense to begin with the main subject of the story: Jesus. This is a practice that Peter Enns recommends in his teaching guide for the curriculum *Telling God's Story*: "We are beginning at the culmination of the story, to see how all of this ends up—acquainting children with the most central truths of the Scripture before we go back to fill in the many interesting details."[5] This may seem like reading the last page of a book and then going back to see how these two people fell in love or why the main character ended up dying at the end. But we must remember that God's story is not an easy story. It's too complex to tell to children—and even adults— linearly. Some episodes are not appropriate for young children, so they can be filed away until they make their appearance at a time when the children are older.

This whole question of which Bible stories are appropriate for children and which are not has riddled Christians throughout history, from early church father John Chrysostom to twentieth-century Catholic theologian Karl Rahner.[6] Sometimes we who minister with children take the tactic that we shouldn't shy away from any Bible story (with very young children being an exception) and sometimes we wimp out and avoid a story or intentionally omit some of the more disturbing or gory details.

Sometimes we avoid some Bible stories because we think they show God in a negative light. Right now Ivy's struggling with how to tell the story of the ten plagues in Egypt and wondering what children will think about God when they learn about the horrible things that happened to the Egyptians at the hands of God. However, a perusal of Hebrew education websites shows that sometimes teaching about the plagues involves celebrating with stickers, play acting masks and small toys. Context is, as they say, everything. What is devastating to the Egyptians is liberating to Israel. Maybe we need to have faith in God's ability to take the questions and doubts that arise when we explore the more violent and disturbing episodes of God's story. Maybe God can take it. Maybe we should think hard before we shy away from telling a biblical story to children just because it can paint an image of God that we may not like.

When we see the Bible as God's story, as a rich and diverse library that tells the complex ongoing story of God's interactions with humanity, we can notice that violent and hostile episodes are often paired with episodes about reconciliation. "The Bible itself, it seems, has built-in reconciling stories to counteract and disarm the hostile ones, but people who want to justify hostility pick the hostile ones and choose to minimize the reconciling ones."[7] Of course, there are stories that are just too disturbing, genocidal or complex to teach to children of certain ages. But when we expose children to the whole of God's story, we can help the puzzle become a picture of reconciliation trumping violence, of love overcoming hatred and of the healing of the world overcoming its hemorrhaging.

Again, this is a complicated issue. It's no wonder that so many people pick which pieces of the puzzle to pass on to children and which to avoid. But we can do better. We can share God's story in a way that doesn't omit or compartmentalize uncomfortable, violent and hostile parts, but shows that God does not reward violence, that kindness is the mark of discipleship and that love wins. Again, this is not easy. Although we may set out to deal with this difficult task, deep inside, we may share Katniss Everdeen's question in the epilogue to *The Hunger Games* trilogy: "How can I tell them about that world without frightening them to death?"[8]

Let's get back to our puzzle analogy. Like the process of putting together the puzzle of Notre Dame de Paris, we begin by telling children the stories of Jesus, by introducing them to the miracles he performed, the teachings he offered, the parables he told and the death he endured. And after a significant period of time (even up to a few years), when the pieces of Jesus' life have all been put together, the time has come to start filling in the rest of the story.

A next step might be to gradually tell children the overall plot of God's story as a way of constructing a frame in which the smaller pieces of the story will fit together. In *The Story We Find Ourselves In*, Brian McLaren breaks the overarching story of God's into seven episodes: creation, crisis, calling, conversation, Christ, church, consummation (also referred to as celebration).[9] Knowing that children would have been exposed to the details of episode five (Christ), it seems appropriate to tell them the CliffsNotes version of the entire story, episode by episode. Like the first step of piecing together the Jesus episode, forming the frame of the story would happen over a significant period of time, during which the main characters and significant plot developments of the story might be told to children.

Finally, once the border has been constructed, the most difficult and time-consuming part of the puzzle begins: filling in the rest of the picture. Slowly but surely, little by little we can tell children the many stories that fill the pages of the Bible, always being careful to make sure that we share them as episodes of the overarching narrative, as pieces of the larger puzzle. This can take a great deal of time, and, in fact, it never ends, for these stories can be told and retold again and again in new and fresh ways as children grow into adolescents and adolescents mature into adults.

When we tell God's story in this way, we can connect pieces of the story in ways we are not able to when it's presented in a piecemeal fashion. For example, the multitude of trees that God planted in Eden (Gen 2:9), particularly the tree of life from which God banished Adam and Eve (Gen 3:22-23), and the trees Ezekiel refers to (Ezek 47:12) are even more abundant in John's vision in Revelation 22:2. In fact, New Testament scholar Brian Blount refers to this scene in Revelation as a description of the "eschatological Eden"—paradise as God intended it to be.[10] And when we share God's story as a unified grand narrative, we share a context for the more disturbing and troubling episodes (like the horror of the plagues in Egypt) that helps us to see the whole of who God is. Questions, complexities and difficulties will still surface. But we'll be better prepared to tackle them with young people when we have an understanding of the whole story.

When we think of God's story as a puzzle, we need to remember that the puzzle is not yet completed. We can never put in the last few pieces. After all, it's an ongoing saga that reaches to us (and beyond us) and extends into the present world. The Bible may give us some clues as to how the story will end, but we are the ones who keep the story going. We are characters, actors and subjects in the ongoing drama of God's interactions with humanity.

In order to describe the ongoing nature of God's story, theologian and New Testament scholar N. T. Wright has likened it to a Shakespearean play that is missing the final act:

> Suppose there exists a Shakespeare play whose fifth act had been lost. The first four acts provide, let us suppose, such a wealth of characterization, such a crescendo of excitement within the plot, that it is generally agreed that the play ought to be staged. Nevertheless, it is felt inappropriate actually to write a fifth act once and for all: it would freeze the play into one form, and commit Shakespeare as it were to being prospectively responsible for work not in fact his own. Better, it might be felt, to give the key parts to highly trained, sensitive and experienced Shakespearian actors, who would immerse themselves in the first four

acts, and in the language and culture of Shakespeare and his time, *and who would then be told to work out a fifth act for themselves.*[11]

We are all actors in God's story—children, youth and adults together are protagonists who tell and retell the story through our lives and are transported into it and become part of this living story. We help direct the storyline and advance the plot.

And since the story has been going on for some time, we can introduce children to characters and episodes that have helped to carry the story from the pages of the Bible to this point in history. We can teach children about the key players in our faith traditions and our own congregations who have advanced the plot to where they entered from stage right. As Ivy has said before, an important part of children's spiritual formation is helping them learn that they are part of an ongoing movement that's existed in all sorts of places around the world for more than two thousand years.[12]

WHEN GOD'S STORY MEETS OUR STORIES

Telling God's story to children is not an end in itself. While it's surely important for children (and adults, for that matter) to gain a solid understanding of God's grand narrative, it's what we do with this story that really matters. When children realize that they are part of this story, that God's story is also their story, that God's story connects with their own expanding self-narratives, they become responsible for ensuring that the episodes in which they make appearances are faithful to the overall script that God has laid out and that they help move the story forward to the concluding eschatological scene.

Christopher Guest (perhaps most famously known as the six-fingered man in 1987 film *The Princess Bride*) has written, directed or starred in a number of "mockumentary" films over the past few decades, including *This Is Spinal Tap*, *Waiting for Guffman*, *Best in Show* and *A Mighty Wind*. Guest has a fascinating way of making films. Often in partnership with Eugene Levy, he writes background material to a film's characters, he outlines the overall plot and he writes particular notes for different scenes. The rest is up to the actors, who move the plot along and add dialogue, action and humor to each scene in ways that are faithful to the overall storyline and in ways that will bring the film to its climax and conclusion. This style of filmmaking is analogous to God's story. While God has given us a sense of the overall plot, the culmination and conclusion of the story, and how we are supposed to act as protagonists in this story, it's up to us—adults and children alike—to fill in the pieces in ways that are appropriate and faithful to God's intentions.

While every congregation, minister, parent and teacher might tell God's story in different ways, we believe that it's helpful for children (at least those who have grown up in the church) to have a good, solid understanding of the story by the time the reach junior high. After all, kindergarten and primary age children learn best through stories. James Fowler, the foremost authority on faith development, believes that this is the time when the "episodic quality of Intuitive-Projective faith gives way to a more linear, narrative construction of coherence and meaning. Story becomes the major way of giving unity and value to experience."[13] We can begin by simply offering stories to young children in imaginative and creative ways, and then by tapping into the growing abilities for logical thought in older children by focusing on facts and more precise details of the narrative.

In an ideal world it would be wonderful if the façade of Notre Dame Cathedral is put together, the border is assembled and even some of the pieces of blue sky are put into place by the time children reach the ages of twelve or thirteen. (This, of course, assumes that the children have been taught about God's story regularly throughout their childhood. If this is not the case, as it often is, then the puzzle will have to be put together in more creative and flexible ways.) In other words, younger children can be introduced to the episodes of Jesus' life, and older children can gain an understanding of the overall plotline of the story, as well as begin seeing where a few key episodes fit in the overall framework. This approach to telling God's story remains true to children's emerging cognitive capacities and phases of spiritual development.

And as the pieces of the puzzle come together, we can help children see how they are living into the story they are learning. Children's ministry involves telling God's story with the hope that children will make the story their own, that they will come to see themselves as actors within the story. As Peter Enns writes, "The goal of this approach is not simply for you or your children to *understand* the Bible. Any teaching of Scripture to children must have a much more practical and deeper purpose: to encourage children to become mature, knowledgeable, and humble followers of Jesus, growing in faith."[14] But how do we who work with children go about doing this? How do we help young people work with the story once they've come to know it and as they grow to know it in new ways?

We know of one church that has adopted an approach that it calls project-based learning. The pamphlet outlining this approach states that "When students are in control of their own curriculum they tend to be more invested in their learning." Thus, project-based learning focuses on ownership, depth, moving beyond intellectual knowledge, using multiple intelligences, and balancing an "inward search with an outward expression."[15]

When children at this congregation reach junior high, it is expected that they've gained some general insight about the story of God, with a particular focus on the life and teachings of Jesus. Although they may not describe their purpose in these words, the junior high Sunday school class uses project-based learning as a way of helping children to live into God's story by engaging in theological reflection and becoming practical theologians.

The process begins in September as the children identify subjects of interest to them. In this planning phase they work together to agree on a topic with a strong religious, spiritual or ethical dimension that will be the focus of the entire year, and they develop a tentative plan for the project, including goals, resources and timelines. One of the recent Sunday school classes chose to spend the year exploring ecology and faith. This first phase can take several weeks to complete.

The second phase is called the discovery phase. Its purpose, according to the pamphlet, is to "explore our topic as deeply as possible and develop a perspective from which we can share our learning." Individually and as a group the students delve into several resources that are relevant to the topic, including biblical texts, church teachings, church history, books and articles, videos, pop culture, websites, interviews and service projects. While studying ecology and faith the class researched many of the economic, ecological, political and theological dimensions of energy consumption and built a theological framework for understanding how to live as custodians of the earth.

After months of researching, exploring and engaging in theological reflection about the selected topic, the final stage of the process begins. During this sharing phase the students "pull together what we have learned into a coherent picture" and present it to other people in the church or the community. They agree on a particular method for sharing what they have learned about their topic and about how it affects their journeys of following Jesus. The class that focused on ecology decided to propose to the wider congregation that it should install solar panels on the roof of their church building. They started a blog to share resources about the issue—including their theological framework—with the congregation and a few members of the class sat on a committee that was formed to explore the possibility of installing solar panels. Eventually the church voted to move forward with this Sunday school class's proposal for producing clean energy.

Project-based learning is certainly not the only way for children to make God's story their own, to help them live into the story in their everyday lives. But it is one creative way of doing so. And, considering that increasing numbers of churches are becoming more committed to active engagement in the world rather than withdrawing from it into isolated islands of Christianity, we imagine that the kind of critical theological reflection that project-based learning helps students do is a welcome approach for churches seeking to do children's ministry in the way of Jesus.

In *The Moral Imagination*, John Paul Lederach writes, "When deep narrative is broken, the journey toward the past that lies before us is marginalized, truncated. We lose more than just the thoughts of a few old people. We lose our bearings. We lose the capacity to find our place in this world. And we lose the capacity to find our way back to humanity."[16] Too often children are not introduced to the deep narrative that is God's ancient-future story that runs through the pages of the Bible and flows into the narratives of our lives. New kinds of children's ministry can rediscover this deep narrative and share it with young people. Let us form children not by offering them random bits of a large picture; let's dump the puzzle onto the table, piece it together with the children in our midst and discern how the pieces of our lives fit into the wider picture.

And when the pieces of the puzzle begin to show the image, to tell the story, we can learn together what it means to live into this story, to follow Jesus more closely by hearing, telling and living God's story.

QUESTIONS FOR CONSIDERATION

1. How does your present ministry with children make connections between different parts of God's story?

2. What nonbiblical stories does your church uphold as important to God's ongoing story (the founding of your denomination or church, a church schism, a change in pastoral leadership and so on)?

3. In what ways does your children's ministry help children enter into God's story in the Bible in such a way that they find connections with their own lives?

4. How can project-based learning help your congregation encourage children to know and live into God's story?

6

Honest Questions

*I never question God. I can only
question my assumptions about God. I only
question my understanding of God.*

PETER ROLLINS, "The Embrace of Unknowing"

◘ ◘ ◘

IVY WAS IN SECOND GRADE, SHE BELIEVES, when she learned that she didn't have the ability to ask good questions. It was time for show and tell and one of her classmates was describing and showing a pet, some kind of lizard. Her teacher encouraged the class to ask questions about the cold-blooded pet and the information that Ivy's classmate was sharing. Ivy raised her hand, a gesture that took a great amount of courage on her part because she was a very reserved child and didn't often participate in class in this way. The teacher called on her, and Ivy asked her classmate where she got his pet. Before her fellow student could answer the question, her teacher jumped in and informed her that this was not an appropriate question. Some fifty years later, Ivy still can't figure out what was so inappropriate about this question to warrant her teacher's insensitive response. Instead of encouraging questions (which the teacher said she was doing), this teacher shut down an already shy child even more. It took years for Ivy to outgrow that moment and feel safe enough to raise her hand to ask questions in a class, seminar or other group setting again.

Children's questions matter. And how we handle their questions matters.

Years after this classroom incident, Ivy was sitting in Burger King with a friend and her young son (who was also in the Sunday school class that Ivy taught). The boy was about three or four years old at the time. He was going through a litany of questions about things God made: Did God make the sun? Did God make the trees? Did God make the flowers? And on and on and on. Finally, he got to his last question: Did God make Burger King? Ivy and the young boy's mother exchanged looks with each other, each one hinting to the other that they weren't quite sure how to answer this question. They tossed around the idea that God made the materials the building was made from and things of that nature. But Ivy doesn't think either one of them ever really answered his question. But it's important that they didn't immediately say, "No. Of course not! God didn't make Burger King," or simply laugh at his question because it was cute and move on to other things. They both attempted to take his question seriously and discuss what God's role might have been in the creation of this fast-food chain. They knew that how they handled children's questions matters.

These stories demonstrate the importance of taking children's questions seriously. How we handle their questions matters because our responses tell them what we think about them and their emerging ideas, theological or otherwise. When we chuckle, shrug our shoulders or tell them that their question isn't good, we say something about who they are and whether or not we value them. Unfortunately, many people can probably recall a time in their younger years (or maybe more recently) when they felt shut down and cast aside because a question they asked wasn't taken seriously.

But when we listen to children's questions and join them in wrestling to find answers, we tell them that they and the things they think are important to us. We tell them that they matter. And we encourage them to keep asking questions. When we treat a child's questions with respect, we are treating the child with respect. And we are teaching him or her that it's okay to ask questions.

As children get older, their questions are less likely to be about reptiles and Burger King, and more likely to be about rules, boundaries and life-defining issues for which we adults might not have adequate answers. Yet honoring and listening to these questions is important too. If we want children to keep talking to us about the things that matter to them, to share their ideas, curiosities and imaginations with us, we ought to respect their questions instead of being disturbed or irritated by them.

For those involved in the spiritual formation of children, it's important to consider how to handle children's questions about matters of faith, religion and spirituality. For those of us who raise, teach and minister with children, it's helpful for us to dig deep and explore our own attitudes toward questions when we are talking to children about God, Jesus, the Bible and other topics. How do we see questions? Does every question a child asks have one absolute, final and true answer? Or is it okay to swim in the paradoxes and ambiguities of faith with children? If we don't have an answer to the question, do we feel like we have failed as teachers, leaders, pastors or parents, or that we don't know enough about faith and the Bible? Are children encouraged to ask questions? Are their answers treated as though they're more important than questions? If a child answers a question with an intriguing but not quite conventional answer, should we explore that answer or hurry to get the child back on the right track? What about questions that disturb us or make us uncomfortable? How we answer these and other questions can help uncover assumptions that can inform us of our attitudes toward children and their questions in the realm of faith. And these types of questions launch us into the subject of this chapter.

QUESTIONING FAITH

In our varied ministry experiences we have seen our fair share of published curricula for congregation-based spiritual formation of children. Although there is a growing number of ministry resources and models being produced that encourage children to question and wonder (Godly Play is a great example), many "big box" curricula include prewritten lessons that provide teachers with an application or a point that students should learn from each lesson.

These lessons often provide questions that test children's knowledge of the factual content of the lesson as well as those that and help generate discussions. These latter questions are typically meant for teachers to ask as a means of helping the class discover the application or main point of the lesson. In all these cases the teacher asks the questions and the students answer them.

While curricula that use questions in this way are a dime a dozen, it's much more difficult to find published curricular resources and ministry models that anticipate for the teacher what questions the children might ask about a particular story or that help the teacher address questions that veer from the suggested path of the lesson. And with the exception of Godly Play and a few other innovative approaches, it can be even more difficult to find resources that help children to ask questions. Published curricula tend to teach children and leaders alike that the point or application offered by a lesson is the meaning of that Scripture passage and that there isn't room for differing interpretations or for asking questions that might unbalance or even discount the intended message of the curricula. Teachers are usually taught to ask questions rather than invite them. And children are usually taught to answer questions instead of ask them.

This is problematic, and for good reasons.

In most curricula, lesson applications or points are typically written as absolutes. The point is a closed case, never open for debate. In these curricula teachers often find statements such as "God will always take care of us" or "God helps us to never be afraid."

Now we don't disagree with these generalized statements. We do believe that God takes care of us and have seen evidence of that in our own lives. And we do believe that trusting in God's care can soften fear and anxiety in our lives.

However, these statements are simplified versions of much more complex, ambiguous and paradoxical theological ideas. We can probably all point to times in our lives when it didn't feel like God was taking care of us or it took a while for us to understand the ways in which God's care was being manifested in a certain situation. And there are certainly times when we've all been afraid despite our cognitive knowledge of God's love for us. These kinds of simplified Bible points don't leave room for nuances found in a life of faith. They seem to express an all-or-nothing, black-and-white, absolute quality to them, which can teach children that these statements will always be true no matter what we might wonder, feel or experience to the contrary.

What young people soon discover, as we and many others have, is that in real life these statements don't always ring true. In real life, things aren't always as simple as what we've been taught to believe. The messiness of life doesn't always work out in ways that make these statements seem true. But we don't tend to tell children and youth this. We may not often offer them opportunities to question these seemingly absolute and factual statements until they are in the throes of some sort of difficulty and are faced with a crisis of faith without tools to navigate it.

What if, instead, we offered young people opportunities to explore more nuanced meanings of how God breaks into our lives by allowing them to dig deep into God's story without burdening this rich narrative with preordained applications? We can help them learn language to describe and discover the work of God in their own lives. We can show them what it means to have a posture of wonder and curiosity instead of absolute and definite answers. And we can teach them that asking questions is as important (maybe even more important) than answering them.

When we do these things, we encourage children to ask questions and provide them with safe spaces to use their knowledge and experiences to read, interpret and even question the Bible. This can help them to understand that a life of faith that leaves room for curiosity is more compelling, interesting and life-giving than one based on short points or lesson applications. When difficult times come, they can have a better understanding of God's ways in their lives and the world.

When children are fed absolutes about faith and how God acts in the world, they might feel a sense of betrayal when life becomes difficult. In tough times they might think that they've been lied to about who God is and what faith is. Perhaps they'll come to think that they're doing something wrong or they'll wonder why God isn't taking care of them the same way they've been told God cares for others. This becomes as good a reason as any for them to leave their childhood faith behind, since the only things that they were ever taught were unnuanced absolutes and they weren't told that it's okay to question what they learned or to go deeper into their explorations of God in the light of real life. In some instances they might have heard teachers say that questioning these unyielding absolute statements is sinful.

Perhaps a better way is to do away with points and lesson applications in our explorations of the Bible with young people and encourage them to ask those questions they are so fond of. Maybe if we just waded into God's story with children, swam around for a bit, and let them lead the way, we would offer them opportunities to interpret the Bible on their own and come up with their own ideas. They can see that the Bible is more than a dusty old book to be studied—it's a story that we are invited to enter into with all our baggage, doubt and questions. And they can learn that God isn't just a divine protector or a wrathful parent, but that God can take our questions and our doubts. After all, if children can do theology, they deserve the freedom to think for themselves about God, the Bible, the world and what it means to follow Jesus, who, by the way, tended to avoid explaining the meaning of his parables and teachings, instead allowing hearers to interpret, make connections and experiment for themselves.

Ivy was guest teaching in a children's ministry course at Christian university in the Midwest. As the class discussed how to teach Bible stories to children, Ivy advocated allowing children to draw their own conclusions about a Bible story by asking questions and creatively entering in to the retelling of the story. The students in the class were intrigued, but shared a concern that the kids might not get to the "right" answer or that they wouldn't be able to find answers to the questions they raise. During this discussion the professor of the course, who was sitting in on the class, spoke up and told the students that he was using this very approach with his Sunday school class every week. He assured them that while he'd had some of their same misgivings when he'd started using this approach, he discovered that the children's questions added vibrancy and interest to the class. In fact, he said that only rarely did he find the need to keep the class on track as the children were very good at finding their own way or self-correcting when needed.

While those of us who teach and lead children may get excited (and a little anxious) about allowing children to explore, question and interact with Bible stories on their own, it's helpful to have someone show us the path. When we know that we're not the first to give children freedom to ask their own questions, we can be reminded of the value of this process to the child's spiritual formation and that it's okay for children to end up somewhere other than where the curriculum tells us they should be.

Let us offer a few glimpses of these ideas. Earlier in this school year Ivy was sharing the parable of the talents with children in her church. Most times that we've seen a curriculum or Bible study explicate this parable, the implications have always been about not wasting the gifts and talents that a person has been given. In the story the investors are seen as industrious, and the servant who protected the gift is seen as cowardly and foolish. But Ivy decided to simply tell the parable to her group of grade school children and see where things went. She was astonished to see that every child in the group questioned the motives of the servants and sided with the one who buried the treasure. According to them, this servant made the prudent and responsible choice while the others engaged in risky behavior with the master's money. They felt that the master was wrong to berate the one who protected his money.

Ivy was astounded and confused by the children's interpretation and the questions they brought to the story. But after taking a minute to think about the cultural context in which these kids are living, things started to make more sense. These children attend a well-established, affluent church in Manhattan, and they're growing up in the aftermath of the global financial meltdown that resulted from a lot of risky behavior with other people's money. They've probably seen firsthand the protests involved in the Occupy Wall Street movement and heard protestors berate financial institutions for playing God with other people's money. With this in mind, no wonder they saw the more prudent servant as the one with the right idea.

If Ivy had tried to teach children a predetermined point of this parable, it wouldn't have rung true for these children. If she'd pushed the conventional application with these youngsters as being "right and true," they may have simply disregarded the story (and perhaps the Bible) as having no relevance to their lives. Or maybe they would've learned that their ideas about the responsibility of the prudent servant weren't true or that they didn't matter. But by allowing them to ask their own questions and draw interesting conclusions in their particular context, they opened up the interpretation of this parable in a new way.

A second illustrative story: Recently Ivy joined children in her church in exploring the story of Jesus calling his "fishermen" disciples. Again, Ivy simply told the story, adding some context about the Sea of Galilee and the fishing industry in early Palestine. She gave the children freedom to raise questions and run with their thoughts about why these men chose to follow Jesus and what it meant for their lives going forward. They talked about the disciples' drop in income and what that meant for their families and whether leaving their livelihood to follow Jesus was like joining a cult. Their questions gave Ivy an opportunity to explore some misconceptions about the Christianity of Jesus and the disciples. None of these topics or questions would have been raised if she'd followed the steps in so many published curricula and tried to get to the prepackaged lesson application.

Sometimes when we share our ideas about giving children freedom to ask questions, people respond by reminding us that all lesson plans need to have a goal, that teachers need to know where they are taking their class, and that they need to know their intended learning outcomes. Otherwise how would a teacher know if they have succeeded?

These statements are absolutely right—if we're talking about school. Lessons ought to have objectives, and there should be some way to evaluate whether a lesson has been successful or not.

However, as we explained in chapter one, school isn't the best way to form someone into a person who loves God and lives in the way of Jesus. As John Westerhoff has argued, a schooling-instructional model of children's Christian education tends to encourage us to assert our power over young students as we seek to make them in our own image, to make them into miniature versions of ourselves, into people who see the world as we see it.[1] His harsh (yet valid) criticism of a schooling-instructional model reminds us that using a story from the Bible or a Scripture passage as a tool to teach a moral, value or virtue as the lesson objective isn't the best way to employ God's story in the spiritual formation of children.

If we take a step back from the schooling paradigm, a whole new exciting world of learning and exploration opens up. We are no longer burdened with the idea that a story or lesson must teach one particular point. We can entertain all sorts of questions from children and discover that we really do care about what they think and that God's story can speak to them in all sorts of ways. And sometimes our interpretations might contradict one another (and that's okay). Parker Palmer eloquently writes about this issue, drawing from the writing of Niels Bohr: "Truth is found not by splitting the world into either-ors but by embracing it as *both-and*. In certain circumstances, truth is a paradoxical joining of apparent opposites, and if we want to know that truth, we must learn to embrace those opposites as one."[2]

WE DOUBT IT

Shortly after Dave started his seminary education, he and his wife, Jenny, were asked to lead the children's program at a weekend camp where Jenny grew up. It had been a while since they'd been at the camp, so they spent a lot of time catching up with people that they hadn't seen since previous summers. During one conversation a senior member of the camp asked Dave what he'd been up to over the summer. Instinctively, he mentioned that he just finished his fourth intensive summer course. Having just discovered that Dave was in seminary, this woman offered some advice, "Be careful. Seminary makes people lose their faith."

This speaks of a fear that some Christians have toward doubt. This woman was genuinely concerned that Dave would doubt his faith by being exposed to new ideas at seminary. And, to a degree, she was right to be concerned. Seminary caused him to doubt and reformulate aspects of his faith.

Luckily, doubt was nothing new for Dave. His faith journey has been one of belief and doubt, two concepts that are often seen as opposing one another but actually complement each other quite nicely. Doubt has always been sneaking up on Dave, making him question, ponder and rethink things that he would come to take as theological certainties. And through these doubts, his faith has grown. Whenever he thinks he's got things figured out, doubt comes in and reminds him that God can never be pinned down.

Anne Lamott once wrote that the opposite of faith isn't doubt—it's certainty.[3] When we are certain about something, we have no reason to have faith. But doubt is difficult. We like to think we have everything figured out, that we know what we believe and that what we believe is true. But we're just fooling ourselves. Peter Rollins writes and speaks about the importance of doubt to an authentic faith:

> To believe is easy. You can fill stadiums with people wanting to believe, either to solidify what they already think or to grasp hold of something because they feel cast adrift and lost at sea. To doubt, to interrogate your fear, to really question what you believe, that's difficult. It's difficult because we want to protect ourselves from doubt and unknowing.[4]

But embracing doubt is often missing in faith communities. We pretend that we've got God, the Bible and our faith all figured out, organized and neatly packaged in a box. This can be particularly true in children's ministry. Even if we have doubts, we don't usually want to pass these on to children. It can even seem like we'd be doing children a disservice by sharing a faith that is littered with doubts.[5]

Ironically, however, it's for this very reason that many young people are leaving the church, or if they make conscious efforts to remain, they often feel isolated.

Dave recently had a speaking engagement at a Christian summer camp in Ontario's Bruce Peninsula. The director of the camp asked him to make the drive north to talk to the summer staff—ranging in age from about seventeen to twenty-three—about having faith-full conversations with campers. As the director gave him a tour of the campgrounds, he told Dave that many of these young camp leaders are on the fringes of their churches. They feel isolated from their faith communities and the wider Christian denomination their churches are a part of. And a major reason for this feeling is that their churches haven't been open to hearing their honest doubts about the Bible, God, church and what it means to be Christian. Their churches are too doubtless for them.

This isn't a particularly unique situation. The findings of David Kinnaman's insightful research (described in *You Lost Me*) show that doubt is one of the major reasons why young adults are walking away from church.[6] But this leaves a question worth pondering: Is doubt a reason young people leave the church, or is it more accurate to say that the church's attitude to doubt is a reason? A fuller reading of Kinnaman's book seems to affirm the latter.

All this goes to show that the church tends to miss the mark when it comes to engaging children and youth in doubts that inevitably arise throughout one's journey of faith. Doubt is more often swept under the rug instead of examined and explored. Young people learn that there's no room for doubt in church, that it's a place for certainty. But this doesn't fit well with the assumptions and attitudes of society. In *unChristian*, Kinnaman reports on conversations and research with young adults who don't count themselves as part of the church. Like several friends we've come to know in recent years, he learns from those who criticize Christianity in order to help the church honestly examine itself. Young people today are, according to him, part of "the ultimate 'conversations generations.' They want to discuss, debate, and question everything. This can be either a source of frustration or an interest we use to facilitate new and lasting levels of spiritual depth in young people."[7]

With this last sentence Kinnaman poses a challenge to the church—to quit being so afraid of young people's doubts, to embrace them, wrestle with them and use them to foster deeper levels of faith and spirituality.

EMBRACING QUESTIONS, DIVING INTO DOUBTS

Young people are growing up in a culture that rejects "Because I said so" as an answer to the why question. They're used to questioning authority, living in complexity and paradox, and holding divergent—even conflicting—attitudes and beliefs at the same time.[8] And for many of them church represents a place where they have to leave all this behind, where they have to settle on one version of truth over another. For many, church is where they're told to stop searching for meaning, where they must stop creatively tinkering with their faith, and where they have to follow the Christian status quo. No wonder so many young people are opting out of the institutional church and even Christianity.

Children's ministry in the way of Jesus sets a place at the table for questions and doubts. After all, the church has always found new life and energy as disconcerted Christians raise questions and express doubts. And today the church is forging fresh ideas and practices for following Jesus as people ask questions about the truthfulness and relevance of more restrictive versions of the faith that they've grown up learning about in Sunday school. And they chose to embrace these questions, to dive into their doubts and to engage in the process of rethinking what it means to be Christian. Many of these spiritual pilgrims found that they had to unlearn what they'd been taught as a child and teen and form a fresh, open, inclusive, just and generous Christianity. And while folks are still sorting out what to hold on to and what to throw out, and while they're not quite sure how to pass on their faith to young people, many agree that they want their children to be curious, questioning Christians who have faith that embraces doubt— or doubt that embraces faith.

Over the years we've seen kids who are consistent church-goers— the ones with the long rows of gold stars showing a near-perfect Sunday school attendance record—reach the tween years and begin complaining that they find Sunday school lessons boring and that they know all there is to know about the Bible. "I already know this story" can be a mantra for some tweens in church. If all their lives these children have been taught that the episodes of God's story are static, with one meaning or application, it's no wonder that they might think there's no reason to explore familiar stories or ideas in new ways.

But children are often naturally curious, and as they grow older, they seem to question everything (even their faith). So while some children might be conditioned by schooling-instructional models of children's ministry to learn the one point of a story or lesson and move on, others will probably have questions or doubts that they want to explore. If we shut down these questions because they make us uncomfortable, because we don't have any answers or because we think it's wrong to question what we "know" about the Bible, we're doing these children a disservice.

If instead, in our churches and our families, we create a culture where we revel in the Bible as God's ongoing story that constantly reveals new things to us, where questions are encouraged and doubts are shared, we may find that children, tweens and teens who are raised in this culture get excited about continuing to delve into ideas about the Bible, God and faith rather than bored by stories and their one-note applications. It creates an environment that balances faith with doubt, understanding with uncertainty. Robert Keeley believes that such an environment helps children's faith to flourish: "Letting children see that we don't have it all figured out gives them permission to live with questions at the same time that they hold on to what they do know—that God loves them and that he is holding them in his hand. This allows their faith to grow so that it doesn't buckle with the first questions."[9]

When we embrace honest, thoughtful and even challenging questions, we can guide children as they deconstruct their faith and reconstruct it ways that allow that faith to seep into their bones, to form the core of their identity, an identity that won't fall apart when doubts arise. The process of asking questions and sharing doubts is one of seeking and searching for truth wherever it may be, and it's this process that leads toward what John Westerhoff calls *owned faith*.[10]

But being open to children's questions and doubts is easier said than done. Earlier in this chapter we posed some questions that help explore how we might react to young peoples' questions about spiritual topics. These questions can help us assess how comfortable we are with young people's questions and doubts. And there are several reasons for being uncomfortable.

For some people questions that seem to draw children away from what we want to impart to them can seem threatening—not only to the integrity of the teaching process but to one's faith. In this situation we may be tempted to ignore them or redirect the question back to where we want to take the lesson. But what if we step back, take a deep breath and listen attentively to the question? Doing so shows respect for the questioner and the questions. What seems threatening at first can become an opportunity to allow children to take us on new trajectories and to learn something new. We don't need to be afraid to let a question or doubt take us off the teachers' guide track. We might just stumble into a discussion that is really meaningful for us and for the children in our midst.

Sometimes we may feel threatened by questions children ask because we might think that we don't know the answer. This is a common concern, and we regularly hear people say things like "But I'm not a Bible scholar! I never went to seminary. I can't answer these sorts of questions." The truth is that people with multiple doctorates and who have studied the Bible and theology for years get asked questions they can't answer (and they may feel even more threatened and anxious—after all, they're supposed to be the experts). Whether you're a seminary professor, a parent or a volunteer teacher, it's important to remember that the life of faith is chock full of questions we can't answer in full—or at all. As one of Ivy's friends so succinctly put it, "that's why we call it faith." So while it's natural to feel anxious when we don't have an answer, we can still take time with children to explore possible answers together. As Rabbi Sandy Sasso once said, "It's not so important that you have an answer. What's important is that you engage in the conversation."[11] And here are three tips for doing so.

First, it can be helpful to ask the question poser to explain the question a little more, to say more about it. We may discover that the questioner isn't asking what we first assumed he or she was asking—and it can give us some time to think of how to engage this question. Second, we can ask the questioner what he or she thinks the answer to the question might be. Children do theology and make meaning on their own, so they may already have an answer or two that they're playing with and for which they're seeking confirmation. Third, we might try throwing the question to the entire class, group or congregation to see what they think about it. This can lead to great discussions.

But sometimes we just have to admit that we don't know the answer. And that's okay. The children will probably respect our openness, candor and honesty. And sometimes children ask questions about faith, God, Jesus and the Bible that we, in the limitations of our humanity, just aren't meant to answer. And we should be truthful with young people about this too.

But what about when young people share their doubts with us? These too can lead to anxiety-ridden and scary moments. After all, don't we share our faith with children so that they develop a robust, genuine faith? To this we answer an emphatic yes! But remember that doubt is part of faith. Being a faithful follower of Jesus means having doubts. The story of "doubting" Thomas is often used to scare children away from having doubts and second thoughts, but a closer look at it reveals that Jesus is willing to accept us with all our questions and doubts. He takes the time to meet Thomas where he is and to help him wrestle with his disbelief (Jn 20:26-29). After all, the Gospels show us that Jesus in his full humanity had a faith that made room for doubt (Lk 22:41-44).

But what if young people's doubts end up leading them to believe something that we didn't intend to pass on to them? This is certainly a risk, but it's a risk that Jesus was willing to take—after all, he rarely explained the points of the parables he told. We can relieve some of our anxiety and fear by remembering that children are on spiritual journeys that began before we knew them and will continue after they leave our care. And sometimes they may wander to places that we'd rather they didn't go. But they need not go it alone. When we create spaces that are safe for young people to share their doubts and disbeliefs, we can remind them that it's all part of having faith, and we can commit to walking with them in these doubts.

One of our favorite parts of teaching people of any age is the questions. Not the ones we ask, but those they ask. Questions make teaching interesting, exciting and challenging. And in this spirit of interest and excitement, Ivy once built an entire confirmation class on questions. The confirmands could ask anything they wanted to about faith, God, the Bible, Jesus or the church, and confirmation leaders would attempt to offer responses and generate discussion. This was always Ivy's favorite class of the confirmation year. As children, youth and adults wrestle together with questions and share their doubts, everyone has opportunities to learn and grow in their quest to follow Jesus.

So let's encourage children to ask questions. Let's open ourselves to hearing their doubts. Let's entertain their alternate interpretations of God's story. Let's be honest about what we believe and what we're not quite sure about. By encouraging questions and wrestling with doubts, children's ministry in the way of Jesus can respect young disciples and honor their burgeoning faith and understandings of Gods.

QUESTIONS FOR CONSIDERATION

1. Where in the life of your congregation are children encouraged to ask questions?

2. What fears or obstacles do you face that might get in the way of allowing children to ask questions and express doubt?

3. Where might there be opportunities for you to make space for questions and doubts in your ministry with children?

4. How can you help the teachers and volunteers in your children's ministry become comfortable with dealing with children's questions and doubts about the Bible, God and their faith experiences?

7

Meaningful Participation

Children, by their presence, invite congregations to make their worship part of the gospel's anti-imperialist counter-narrative by prioritizing accommodations to the "least and littlest" among them. . . . One of the most important gifts children bring to a congregation's worship life is the opportunity to act and look like the radically welcoming community of Jesus whether or not a profit can be made, whether or not there is any apparent benefit to the bottom line. A *congregation seeking to welcome children (and in doing so, welcome Jesus and the One who sent him) may or may not increase its membership rolls or treasury, but it surely increases its faithfulness.*

JOYCE ANN MERCER, *Welcoming Children*

▣ ▣ ▣

JANICE, EMILIO AND TORY ARE THREE PASTORS who regularly meet for conversation over coffee and pastries at a local donut shop in the downtown core of their city. Each Tuesday, they share their pastoral concerns with one another, celebrate recent accomplishments and offer mutual encouragement and advice.

On one particular Tuesday, Tory arrived late and looked especially frustrated when he sat down at the table.

"What's the matter?" Emilio inquired.

"You look like I do when I come home from our parish board meetings," joked Janice.

"I'm at my wit's end," Tory responded. "Two weeks ago we discovered a colony of bats living in the church's attic. We've tried everything to get them out: we climbed on the roof after they left for the night, hoping to plug the entrance they discovered. But we couldn't figure out how they were getting in. The administrator called an exterminator, but whatever he did didn't seem to work, because they were back in the attic three days later. I just don't know what to do anymore."

"Oh, we had the same problem a few years ago," Janice replied. "There's something about old, dusty church attics that seem to attract the little critters."

Tory perked up. "Well, how did you get rid of them?"

"Easiest thing in the world: we baptized and confirmed them. They never came back to church again!"

This humorous fictional story points to a reality that far too many faith communities face. No, it's not bats in the attic. It's the mass exoduses of young people when they reach adolescence and adulthood. Whether a church practices infant baptism and confirmation or infant dedication and believer's baptism, ministers see the truth of this joke as attendance rates for young people drop off as children become teenagers and teenagers grow into adulthood.

For many faith communities, this trend of a high dropout rate for adolescents and young adults begins in Sunday school, as children join one another in church classrooms to learn about Scripture, seasons, sacraments and what it means to be Christian. Of course, learning about these and other common Sunday school topics is fundamental to the development and articulation of Christian faith. What we learn in Sunday school often becomes the building blocks for the faith that forms and reforms throughout our lives.

But there's an inherent problem with Sunday school as it is commonly practiced: in order to learn about the basics and fundamentals of the faith, children are often sequestered from the rest of the faith community. This is particularly true if Sunday school (or children's liturgy or whatever a children's program might be called) happens at the same time as a congregation's worship service. In essence, in our efforts to nurture Christian faith in our children, we end up creating a separate community that is distinct and often isolated from the wider body of believers who participate in worship services and other core practices of the faith community.

Now, imagine a child who has grown up in the church but has never really been a part of the core community. Sure, this child may recall a few times when she got to sit with her parents or guardians during congregational worship or the annual church picnic, where the whole community seemed to come together as one. But, for the most part, much of her childhood church experiences were largely removed from the wider faith community and took place in separate spaces, whether in the church's nursery, the colorful preschool classroom or one of several age-based Sunday school classrooms. Maybe she even got to hang out in the youth room when she finally started junior high! She may very well have a veritable storehouse of wonderful memories as she was surrounded by good friends and kind Sunday school teachers her whole life.

But now she has grown too old for children's church, she's graduated from Sunday school and has finally become one of the oldest teens in the youth group. The time has come for her to join the wider congregation in the church's worship service.

At first it's exhilarating being in the service. She spends a lot of time figuring out when to stand, sit, kneel and sing. She learns new hymns and belts out the ones she already knows. She tries hard to listen to the sermons or homilies, remembering the Bible stories she learned throughout her tenure in Sunday school. She feels like an adult—and it feels great!

But after a while she starts to daydream during the sermons, which speak about careers, family life and marriage—things which are so far in the future that it's hard for her to imagine how the message relates to her life. The sound of the organ starts to get annoying. The pattern of sit-stand-kneel, sit-stand-kneel, sit-stand-kneel has lost its novelty and is now predictable and dull, especially when this young woman recalls the hilarity of youth group games, the sweet and tasty treats she would win during weekly sword drills, and the feeling of sheer enjoyment during a rousing game of Duck, Duck, Goose. Oh, the memories!

It's no wonder, then, that as young people like this girl grow too old for Sunday school (or, in keeping with the joke that began this chapter, when they finish confirmation classes), many opt out of church. With the familiar territory of the Sunday school classroom or the youth room only a memory, young people who finally find themselves surrounded by the wider faith community are like strangers in a foreign land. The music is different, the rituals are confusing and their meanings are unclear, and it seems that nothing is like it was when they were kids. It's basically a new church for them, and it's one that many decide to leave.

WHAT WE'RE NOT SAYING

Before we go on to explain what we're saying with this description of what it might be like to grow up in a particular faith community, let's take a moment to address what we're *not* saying.

We're not saying that going to church is synonymous with following Jesus. In fact, we've heard countless stories of folks who've had negative experiences with churches and end up leaving a faith community because it doesn't seem to promote a radical, authentic, life-giving journey of following Jesus. To continue being disciples they've had to walk away from particular churches and seek out other, more creative, authentic and organic communities. So leaving church doesn't necessarily mean turning away from a commitment to follow in the way of Jesus. But at their best the two concepts are difficult to separate completely. After all, being a disciple of Jesus is an arduous journey and requires the continual support and mentorship of other disciples — regardless of age. Sadly, however, too many young people who decide that it's time to move on from church also decide that it's time to move on from Jesus.

We're also not saying that Sunday school, children's church, youth group and other activities and programs for young people shouldn't be fun. Play, laughter and fun are important ingredients in the building of strong relationships and in the forming of lasting memories of positive experiences — all important to the formation of young disciples. However, too much emphasis on fun can lead to a neglect of other vital aspects of strong relationships and significant experiences, like wonder, awe, intrigue, love, curiosity, astonishment, kindness, compassion, honesty, humility and even the challenges of struggle and doubt.

And we're not saying that worship services are boring and irrelevant. With the incredible variety of forms, shapes and sizes of worship services—from small and silent Quaker meetings to enormous Pentecostal services with passionate music and preaching, from the reverence embedded throughout Orthodox or Catholic Mass to the liturgical traditions that characterize worship in many mainline traditions—it's impossible to make generalized statements about worship services being the cure for a tough case of insomnia. In fact, countless people find times of worship with their faith communities to be life-giving and inspiring catalysts of power and energy to continue being hope-filled, world-changing contemplative-activist Jesus followers.

We're not saying that separate programs for children and youth ought to be utterly abolished. It's a sociobiological reality that people of different ages learn and experience the world in different ways. And this ought to be taken into consideration when developing practices for nurturing children's spiritual lives. For example, many congregations rely (with good reason) on James Fowler's theory of faith development. But it is wise to keep in mind, as Robert Keeley cautions readers as he attempts to educate them about this theory, that theories of human development are flawed and limited—sometimes in ways that we are unable to articulate or pinpoint.[1]

Although theories of cognitive, moral and faith development have come under scrutiny, it's difficult to deny that children learn differently from youth, and that young people who are just beginning their adult lives often perceive reality and take in information in ways that differ from that of older adults who are nearing the end of life. There's a place, therefore, for Christian education programs and activities that separate children from adults and even break them into age-specific classes or groups, much like public elementary school systems.

While age-segregated programs and activities for children serve important purposes, too often they become the most common—if not the only—way for children to participate in the life of the church. The problem, however, is that this can hardly be called participation in the faith community. It can seem more like the formation of a separate, kids-only faith community. In fact, we've even seen churches that not only have separate kid-friendly spaces but also separate entrances to church buildings that are to be used for parents to drop off children to go to Sunday school and then pick them up again after the grown-ups participate in congregational worship.

It's no wonder then that children and adolescents who "graduate" from these types of programs often don't continue showing up for worship services and don't choose to be part of a congregation any more. After all, for much of their lives they were part of another faith community, one that met in the basement, the Sunday school wing, the children's pavilion or the youth room.

While it's easy to place the blame for this sort of predicament squarely on the shoulders of clergy and church leadership, we've seen parents become complicit in this exodus by using nonattendance in worship service as a bargaining chip for keeping their child involved in the church's youth group or children's program. As parents tell their children to hurry up before they're late for church, the child might say something like "But I went to youth group on Friday night. I've already been to church this week." (Note the equation of attendance at the youth group with attendance at worship services.)

After several weeks of pouting and skirmishes, this argument can begin to make sense to parents, especially since their child is not completely disconnecting himself from the church. Perhaps if the church had helped this child participate in the community from the beginning, if it had helped both parent and child feel a strong sense of belonging and connection to this faith community, the young person may have come to value involvement in the congregation and he or she would be the one dragging the parent to church. (Hey, we're hopeful!)

Toward Participation

We believe that children matter to the life of the church. We believe that the church can only be the people of God when members—including the youngest—participate in its life, engage in core practices and exercise their gifts as vital members of the body of Christ.

But to participate in the life of the faith community, children need to be part of this community. And to be part of the community, they need to be present for its central practices. They need to rub shoulders with all sorts of folks who make up this community. They need to witness and participate in what exactly it is to be a member of Grace Presbyterian Church, St. Theresa's Catholic Church or Oakwood Community Church. They need to be seen as active and valued members of their faith community. And when they participate in meaningful ways in the core practices that define a faith community, they can allow these experiences to penetrate their bones and help them grow not only as members of a particular church but as members of the band of misfits seeking to follow in the way of Jesus.

What we're saying here isn't anything new, even if it's not heard often enough. There's biblical precedent for children's participation in the core practices that make up a community of faith.[2] And contemporary sociological research buttresses this precedent by demonstrating the necessity of apprenticing young people into a community through their participation in central practices.

Participation in the Bible. The book of Exodus recounts the story of Moses giving instructions to the Israelites on the eve of the twelfth plague, right before he is to lead Israel out of Egypt. He concludes by imploring Israel to commemorate this historic event in a ritual, which serves to teach children about what is about to happen on this particular night. Moses says, "And when your children ask you, 'What does this ritual mean to you?' you will say, 'It is the Passover sacrifice to the LORD, for the LORD passed over the houses of the Israelites in Egypt. When he struck down the Egyptians, he spared our houses'" (Ex 12:26-27).

And as the story of God's relationship with Israel continues, we come upon a similar passage in the book of Joshua. After leading Israel across the Jordan River, Joshua constructs at Gilgal a monument of twelve stones that the tribes of Israel had picked from the waters of the river. Then he turns to the people of Israel and says, "In the future your children will ask their parents, 'What about these stones?' Then you will let your children know: 'Israel crossed over the Jordan here on dry ground'" (Josh 4:21-22).

As the epic saga of God's interactions with humanity continues, the spotlight shifts to the communities of early Christians that sprang up across the Roman Empire. In a letter to the church at Ephesus, the writer (traditionally credited as Paul) encourages children to follow the commandment to honor one's mother and father (Eph 6:1-3). Without going into detail about the important fact that the writer takes time to address children, it's important to note that this writer seems to assume that children will be present among these Christians upon the reading of this letter.[3]

In each of the stories children are present to participate in the life of their faith communities. They participate in rituals, commemorate events at religious memorials and are with the community on opening night for what was to become one of our contemporary lectionary readings. They aren't whisked away to children's church Ephesus-style where they learn about Passover and the parting of the Jordan in age-based classrooms. Biblical scholar Patrick Miller says it best when he writes that in these ancient teachable moments "instruction of the child is not simply in a classroom. It is highly contextual, growing out of context and practice. The religious and social practices of the community, when carried out in continuing and regular fashion, become the occasion for the young ones to learn who they are and whose they are."[4]

So there's nothing new about engaging children in the practices that define the core life of the faith community. The Israelites did it. The Ephesians did it. And now the baton has been passed to our generation. Will we take this gift that is handed to us and run with it?

Turning to sociology. Sociologist Barbara Rogoff explores human development as a process that is deeply entwined within the cultural realities of human beings. Central to her ideas is the perspective that "Humans develop through their changing participation in the sociocultural activities of their communities, which also change."[5] Learning and formation occur, then, not only through observation windows or in age-specific classrooms (although these learning contexts are important), but most significantly through involvement in the practices of a community. It's often held that Kong Qiu (more commonly known by his Westernized name, Confucius) once said, "I hear and I forget. I see and I remember. I do and I understand." Two thousand five hundred years later, sociologists like Rogoff are confirming his words.

Taking Rogoff's ideas to heart, faith communities need to open themselves to the involvement of children in the activities and practices that define their community life. Certainly, this means inviting young people to participate in the rituals and symbolic actions that are part of a church's worship life: baptisms, Scripture reading, reciting creeds, Communion and Eucharist, foot washing, special holy days, hymn singing, and much more. But churches have other defining practices as well. Hosting community events, volunteering at Out of the Cold programs or food banks, sharing meals at potlucks and picnics, writing letters to politicians, pausing to celebrate and mourn together, advocating for safe public housing, being involved in community organizations, making decisions that will guide the church—activities like these are just as vital to the life of a congregation as those that have a more overt and traditionally religious tone.

Coming to terms. In the past we've both written about the importance of welcoming children into congregations.[6] However, as our thinking has evolved, the word *welcome* seems increasingly problematic for conveying our hopes and wishes for children and the church. *Welcome* speaks of an insider doing the welcoming and an outsider being welcomed. Hosts welcome guests. Citizens welcome visitors. Families welcome strangers. But in faith communities, shouldn't children already be seen as family members rather than as strangers? These young ones that Jesus held up as exemplary members of God's reign are certainly not guests, visitors or strangers in the kingdom of God. So who are we to treat them as outsiders to our faith communities? (Maybe they're the ones who should be extending their hands and welcoming us into the kingdom.)

So what is a more appropriate word? *Invite? Embrace? Include?* Each of these words fails to fully hold children as legitimate community members. Each word assumes an active and a passive role. Someone actively invites, embraces or includes while another is passively invited, embraced or included.

Maybe *participate* is a better word. Or *engage*. Or *share*. Or *belong*. Or *interact*. These verbs don't automatically place one party in the dominant active role and the other in a submissive or passive role. Many people can participate, engage and share together. They can belong to one another. These words speak of human *beings*, of people who actively *are* and *do* together. And they move us toward views of children and adults being church together, of offering and receiving invitations to participate with one another.

Multiple communities. As with most things in today's world, nothing is as simple as it first seems. While the fact that human beings develop through meaningful participation in communities of practice seems simple enough, there's more to it than this. Children surely ought to be members of church communities. But they're also members of other communities and are being apprenticed into other ways of living, thinking and being. And these communities often coexist, compete and even intermingle in the lives of children. Rogoff writes, "individuals often participate simultaneously in several different communities. Increasingly, the boundaries between inside and outside are blurred as people spend time in various communities."[7]

The pervasiveness of so many different communities vying for the fidelity of children and youth is one reason why some young people might opt out of being part of a Christian community. Other communities and organizations in society are spending countless dollars to gain children's loyalty, and in many cases they do a much better job at attracting and maintaining it. For example, in our consumption-based culture, children are valuable assets to corporations, since they can develop lifelong brand loyalty from an early age. Just think of the success Disney has had with its Princess line, often getting toddlers on board with their intentional strategies for developing brand loyalty and then re-releasing films from a nonexistent "vault" in order to target adults with fond memories of watching these films during childhood. Without intentionality on the part of faith communities, young people can easily choose to be part of other communities while pushing the church (and oftentimes Jesus) to the sidelines.

A GRADUAL PROCESS

The participation of children in the practices that define the Christian faith in a particular denomination, tradition or community is consistent with the view of children we've offered throughout this book. Since children's spiritual capacities allow them to know God, they should be considered true and meaningful members of communities that gather to worship God and scatter to infiltrate the world with God's love. Since they are disciples-in-training (as we all are), they should be apprenticed into activities carried out by disciples of Jesus.

But even though children are spiritual beings, even though they know God, even though they think theologically and even though they can be disciples, the truth is that they're still fairly new disciples. So, like anyone apprenticing a newbie into a career, we shouldn't throw too much at children at once.

In their book *Situated Learning*, Jean Lave and Etienne Wenger put forth a theory of learning they call legitimate peripheral participation.[8] They hold that learning happens as people participate in communities of practice, particularly as newcomers rub shoulders with old-timers. But newcomers aren't just thrown into the mix of activities that are more difficult or might require the experience of old-timers. They begin with more basic activities that, while important to the community, are less complex and more manageable for the knowledge and skill levels of newcomers. For example, a new coffee shop barista doesn't start her first shift by making a venti nonfat decaf caramel macchiato with half-foam and heated to the perfect temperature. The trainee begins with learning about the different equipment at the coffee shop, practicing how to take and ring up orders, measuring ingredients for pastries, and slicing vegetables for sandwiches, and observes fellow employees perform more difficult tasks. When the trainee is ready, he can try his hand at the more complex activities that he's observed.

It's similar for churches. While we may want children to be full participants in faith communities, their relative inexperience means that participation ought to be gradual, beginning with more simple and manageable tasks. But participation shouldn't end here. As children develop the skills and language to master relatively basic activities, more seasoned disciples can continue mentoring them by allowing them to observe and—when the time is right—engage in activities that are gradually more complex, difficult and challenging. Perhaps young children can be paired with their parents or other adults to greet people arriving for worship. Maybe kids can hold bread during Communion while an adult mentor stands beside them with the cup. Young people can be invited to help prepare a meal for a homeless shelter, and later share it with those it was prepared for. And the possibilities for apprenticing children into the community of Christ followers go on and on. But in each practice and with each activity, children's learning is situated within the practices of the faith community. They learn by engaging in practices that define what it means to be a disciple of Jesus in a particular community, tradition or context.

Pitching in. Children can begin their apprenticeship into the practices of a faith community by pitching in with existing practices and activities. Based on their interests, skill levels and talents, children can lend a hand in collecting the offering, folding bulletins, serving food at community meals, maintaining the church's gardens or green space, and several other activities that contribute to the life and vitality of a congregation.

The idea of children as "consumers" of church activities who take in what congregations have to offer—instead of pitching in with the tasks and activities that need to be accomplished in all areas of community life—is a relatively new phenomenon. Prior to the boom in industrialization in the 1800s and 1900s, "children collaborated with family members in the more varied family work as well as social life that was common before the division of labor of factory life."[9] And as they lent a hand, they learned about the community that was gradually nurturing them into becoming full participants and contributors.

Guided participation. Another level of children's involvement in a faith community is guided participation. Young people are led by more experienced peers or adults as they contribute together in activities and practices. Instead of lending a hand in more basic tasks, children engage in practices and activities that they wouldn't necessarily be able to accomplish on their own. This process of coordination and communication through participation in shared practices is fundamental to human development.[10]

There are countless ways to encourage children's development as members of this Christ-following community through guided participation. Adults can guide children in preparing and serving Communion, in organizing service initiatives like collecting food for a local food bank in lieu of trick-or-treating on Halloween, in working with infants or toddlers in the church's nursery, in visiting congregation members who are shut-ins, in building houses with Habitat for Humanity, in planning prayers, texts and songs for worship services, and in many other ways. Whatever practices or activities are part of your faith community, think about how to help children engage in them through guided participation with more experienced peers or mentors. As children are guided in practices just beyond their current level of competency, the opportunities for growth are significantly enriched.

Equal to serve. We've seen that Rogoff's research into how different societies help children develop can inform how faith communities can encourage children's participation. But it can only take us so far. Churches ought to treat children with more respect and more appreciation than anyone else in society.[11] This means doing more than having kids pitch in, and it means something greater than guided participation—although involvement at these levels is important. It means treating children as equals on the journey to follow Jesus. It means making the church an equal-opportunity community, where children have as much say in the shape and life of the church as adults do.

What would happen if we began treating children as equals on our mutual quests to follow Jesus? Children would have a voice, a vote and a stake in the faith community. They could initiate fundraising campaigns to build schools in an impoverished region of the world, help pay for medical supplies for a family struggling to support their child who is undergoing ongoing medical treatments, take a bite out of hunger in their community or abroad, or another project of their choosing. Perhaps young people can be asked to not only read Scripture but to prepare and offer sermons or even lead whole worship services—but in ways of their choosing. Maybe a few children and adolescents can be welcomed onto church councils or boards to represent the voice of young people within the decision-making processes of the congregation. Instead of asking how children can help us, this level of participation allows adults to pass the baton to young people or, better yet, to carry the baton hand-in-hand with children as we run the race together.

In a culture that tends not to give children a voice (beyond influencing their family's purchases), ideas and practices like these are countercultural. But they're consistent with the respect and value attributed to children throughout the epic narrative of God.

CHANGING COMMUNITIES

Children don't always do things according to our adult expectations of them. They can be noisy, messy, forgetful and overexcited. They can have trouble sitting still, listening quietly or paying attention. All of these fairly common characteristics of children don't seem to make them the ideal candidates for joining adults in worship services. It's no wonder that goldfish crackers and Cheerios have to be picked up from the floor each Sunday, and action figures or comic books need to be returned to their owners. Congregational worship services aren't really set up for children. In fact, some of the more common and central practices and activities of faith communities aren't terribly child-friendly.

We're not saying that worship services should be fun and entertaining. The last thing that children need in our consumer-based, novelty-seeking culture is more glitter and glam vying for their attention. But we are saying that adult expectations of worship and other practices aren't very conducive to the participation of children. When it comes down to it, children have needs that can conflict with those of adults in the liturgical life of a congregation.[12]

So if church practices aren't usually planned and formed with children in mind, their participation is probably going to disrupt things. One of Dave's friends recently told him about a church he visited that handed over to the children the task of collecting the offering. In a church that was used to having adult volunteers silently walk down the aisle with offering baskets in hand while congregants listened to contemplative music as they waited for the basket to reach them, the children definitely changed it up. It was noisy and somewhat chaotic as four or five children quickly walked up and down the aisles in holy disorder. Some people were never handed the offering basket while others had two or three children passing it to them. But in the end, no one seemed to mind. In fact, the congregation appreciated the fact that its children were taking leadership roles. The children were not only involved in this practice, but they offered leadership to it without being told how to collect the offering by adults. This is a fine example of how children can actively and meaningfully participate in a faith community according to their gifts and abilities rather than those of adults.

In chapter two we spoke about opening ourselves to the wisdom and spiritual gifts of children. This is incredibly important as we help them participate in the central practices of our faith communities. As a faith community opens itself to meaningful participation of children, things are going to change. In their important book *Children in the Worshiping Community*, David Ng and Virginia Thomas say that even though children and adults have different abilities and attitudes, they each have gifts to bring to worship: "A vital element in all ages worshiping together is this wedding of adult and childhood gifts in our corporate liturgy. Our differences become a rich harmony."[13] As young people offer leadership to us, their fellow spiritual pilgrims, they lead us to worship God and be God's church in new ways. Since they walk along the spiritual journey—since they are quite capable of knowing God—they have much to teach and share with us.

This is a truth that growing numbers of forward-thinking Christians are embracing. Teachers, leaders, pastors and parents like Carla Barnhill are helping us see that there is

> tremendous value in allowing children not only to be themselves but to *bring* themselves to the community. Rather than seeing children as somehow unfinished and unable to participate in the life of the church until they have learned something, we can encourage children to contribute to the community. When we treat them like full and essential members of the community, we allow their *Imago Dei* to shine through.[14]

Too often we adults assume that children should enter our practices, that is, those meant to serve the spiritual needs of adults. But as we watch children like those who haphazardly yet meaningfully collected the Sunday offering, we learn that we need to enter practices that they invite us to participate in. When we do this, the silence, solitude, contemplativeness and quiet reverence often held up as most appropriate for prayer and worship is nuanced with the holy awkwardness of noise, confusion, conversation, disruption and disorder.

We dream of a local church that is willing to radically rethink what it means to worship God together in ways that are meaningful across generations. This wouldn't mean simply tweaking our current elements of worship to make them more child friendly, and it wouldn't involve the juvenilization of the church. Instead it would mean turning a fresh page, starting over and rethinking what it means for a group of committed disciples of all ages to worship God together. As the contemporary world brings new ways of thinking about and doing church together, we hope this is part of the agenda.

In her book *Welcoming Children*, Joyce Mercer asks, "what would happen if, instead of removing children for not conforming to the styles of worship comfortable for adults, we changed some of those styles to invite the fuller participation of children?"[15] We imagine Jesus would answer this question by taking a child into his arms and saying, "The kingdom of God belongs to such as these." Will we follow our teacher?

QUESTIONS FOR CONSIDERATION

1. Name some ways your church engages children in their practices. How can these examples be used to help your faith community embrace and be more proactive about helping children more fully participate in the community of faith?

2. What current practices are central to your congregation? How can you more fully engage children in these practices? How can children offer leadership to these practices?

3. In what ways might children reshape and reimagine current practices in your church or ministry?

4. What roadblocks do you perceive you might face in efforts to more fully engage children in your church's core practices?

8

Radical Hospitality

As a committed Christian, I have always struggled with locked doors—
doors by which we on the inside lock out "the others"—Jews, Muslims,
Mormons, liberals, doubters, agnostics, gay folks, whomever. The more
we insiders succeed in shutting others out, the more I tend to feel locked
in, caged, trapped.

BRIAN McLAREN,
Why Did Jesus, Moses, the Buddha, and Mohammed Cross the Road?

▫ ▫ ▫

IVY IS AN INTROVERT, AND IT HAS dogged her all of her life.
Being an introvert is often misunderstood. People think introverts are
shy and aloof. This is not necessarily so. Introverts like Ivy get their
energy from being alone; they need their space in order to recharge.
Since groups of people tire them out, they typically prefer one-on-one
interactions. And generally they despise making small talk. They
usually take time to process things and aren't often the first people to
speak up in group settings. For these reasons, sometimes people think
that introverts are indecisive or timid.

As Ivy looks back on her life as an introvert, she can identify times
when she has felt left out, ostracized and, yes, even discriminated
against in evaluations of her job performance because of her introversion. And one of these places she's felt this is the church. Over the

years she has honed her ability to play the role of the extrovert in order to get along and get the job done, but even as a child she longed deep inside for her solitude and simply to be left alone. She so wishes that churches would welcome her in her introversion—to understand and respect her for it and to respectfully call her on it when it gets in the way of communal life and healthy relationships. But sadly, she's found few churches that seem to make room for introverts like her.

We're sure everyone can name a time during childhood when they felt excluded for one reason or another. Maybe it had to do with gender or sexual orientation, the color of one's skin or a person's cultural background; one's accent, native language or place of birth; one's personality, age, abilities, learning style, interests; . . . the list goes on and on. But whatever the reason, we bet folks will agree that being excluded hurts. It can cause wounds and pain that may take years to heal—and may never heal entirely. And when exclusion happens in churches, in communities that are supposed to be open and welcoming, it cuts even deeper.

Children's ministry in the way of Jesus makes room for all sorts of diversity through spaces of radical hospitality. In this chapter we address how children's ministry can become places where all children can be accepted and find belonging. We address how to create ecclesial environments for children's ministry that are places of radical hospitality, places where all young people are welcomed for whom they are and not whom we hope they will become, places where children who are weary from being labeled different can come and find rest.

ROOM FOR ALL

Several years ago Ivy read an article in a well known children's ministry magazine extolling the virtues of a particular organization that was running a Sunday evening program which proved to be quite successful in attracting large numbers of children. One of the features of this program was the wild and crazy games they played each week. Sometimes they even had food fights. Now, the folks who ran this program were aware that there might be families who wouldn't want their children's clothes destroyed in a food fight or a messy game. So as the children arrived on nights when their clothes were at serious risk, those who weren't allowed to participate in the messy games received a special sticker so the volunteers knew they shouldn't get their clothes dirty. So the children with a sticker sat out on the fun.

This idea is wrong on multiple levels. (We won't even get into the ethics of wasting food in a church-sponsored food fight when hunger is such an issue in our world.) But for the purposes of this chapter, we'll focus on the stickers. By promoting a game from which some children needed to be excluded, this church was creating, to be fairly blunt, two classes of youngsters. As Ivy read this article, all she could think about was how the children with the stickers must have felt as they watched their friends participate in the crazy, messy games. She was sure that some children probably really enjoyed the game. But what about those who had to sit on the sidelines? Did they feel left out? Did they feel like something was wrong with them? Were they angry at their parents because they wouldn't let them play the games? What kind of message was this sending about loving God and living in the way of Jesus? And what about those kids who don't like loud, noisy games and large groups? What was happening to them? What kind of impression of the community of faith were they getting through these activities? Of course, this is a very mild form of exclusion, but it provides a clear example of how children's ministry may not always offer hospitality to all young people. And sometimes it can be downright exclusive.

Too often, churches hold stereotypical views of children. They can buy into stereotypes and generalizations that kids are happiest when they are running around (or even that they *need* to run around all the time), that children always make lots of noise, that they crave constant entertainment, or that they have the most fun when they're on the verge of being out of control. But by viewing each unique child through stereotypes and labels we attach to them, children's ministry can become co-opted by consumerist, market-driven agendas, and it forgets the church's mission of offering radical hospitality to the least of these. It may be easier to engage in children's spiritual formation when we assume that they all have the same needs, proclivities and interests, but we remain faithful to the way of Jesus, who took a child into his arms and saw her for the unique person she was, when we offer radical hospitality to children for who they are, regardless of their race, interests, socioeconomic background, gender and so on.

Although the subject of hospitality, when addressed in relation to children's ministry, is often limited to the issue of children with special needs, it is in reality a much broader concern. It includes those issues discussed in the opening paragraphs of this chapter as well as countless other reasons for why children might be excluded or left on the sidelines. Most people who minister with children would certainly go out of their way to make sure a child with a disability is always able to fully participate. But we don't always know what to do with children who are quiet, who aren't athletically gifted, who are particularly bright, who seem to struggle to understand what the other children pick up in no time, who emigrated from another part of the world (or even another part of our countries or cities), or who haven't really been to church before.

Each child is unique. Like all human beings, children have likes, dislikes, proclivities, preferences and personality traits that combine to make up the distinct persons that they are. There can never be one ministry, program or initiative that perfectly fits every single child. Although we may find it easier to create one-size-fits-most ministries for young people, this doesn't respect the particularities and uniqueness of each child—especially those who for one reason or another tend to find themselves excluded from groups and activities in other settings.

This situation may actually have more to do with the adults who organize and lead children's ministry. Perhaps those of us who are creating and managing ministry initiatives with children are more apt to do so using strategies, methods and models that we are comfortable with. If a person tends to like events that are loud and crazy or is convinced that this is what is good for children, this person is probably more likely to create spaces for children that reflect these preferences and views. If a leader is uncomfortable with activities that seem on the verge of chaos or if this person is more quiet or contemplative than others, he or she might be more likely to push activities, programs and classes that speak to children who share this outlook.

Those responsible for facilitating the spiritual formation of children would do well to be aware of our own biases. We do well to realize that in order to extend God's radical hospitality to all children, we need to sometimes move out of our own comfort zones, get beyond our personal preferences and particular ways of life, and take a closer look at what we do. We need to ask ourselves what our ministry with children (every part of it, not just the content) teaches young people about what it means to be a person who follows Jesus. We need to explore how what we do helps nurture the souls of the children involved and how it might exclude some children in the process. And to help spark this process, we'll share ideas surrounding a few categories of difference. Of course, other categories matter as well, but we include these three because they have been particularly important to us in our ministry with children.

LEARNING AND INTELLIGENCE

Children learn in different ways, and there are several ways to talk about various learning styles. One understandable way is to speak of three broad styles: visual, auditory and kinesthetic, or learning primarily through eyes, ears and movement. While children can certainly learn in all three ways, they also often have a preferred or dominant learning style. A person who prefers to learn visually is still able to learn through hearing or movement; this just means that they learn best or are more comfortable learning visually. Working to ensure that all learning styles are present in children's ministry is an act of radical hospitality, of opening wide the arms of the church and creating space for all children—regardless of preferred learning style—to feel comfortable and learn however they prefer to do so.

Another way of understanding different ways that children learn is through multiple intelligences (MI). For the last few decades Howard Gardner has been researching and writing that there is not a one-size-fits-all type of intelligence.[1] Some people have a linguistic intelligence, a musical intelligence or a logical-mathematical intelligence. Others possess a spatial, interpersonal, intrapersonal (introspective), bodily-kinesthetic or naturalistic intelligence. Practitioners in their zeal to make this discovery practical have tried to turn these intelligences into another type of learning style, but this isn't what MI theory is really about. Basically, it means there are different ways of being smart. Human beings have different ways of processing and mentally representing information they are given. And this results in certain kinds of products or performances reflective of one's dominant intelligence. For example, a student with a dominant musical intelligence can certainly learn factual information about history, but this student might not do well on a written test. However, if given the chance to write a song about a historical event or that reflects the emotions surrounding an historical event, the student can better demonstrate his or her knowledge and reflection about historical material.

Unfortunately, most schools in our culture favor a linguistic and logical-mathematical way of being smart, so essays and standardized tests almost always trump ways of evaluating that take other intelligences into consideration. And therein lies an implication of multiple intelligences. We need to understand that children who don't fit into culturally prescribed intelligences are still smart and have much to offer the wider community. There are no tests or metrics for the multiple intelligences, and there may never be. But, as with learning styles, if we pay attention to these diverse ways of being an intelligent being, we may become aware of the types of intelligences represented in the groups of children in our midst.

ABILITY

Much has been written about creating hospitable ministries for children with special needs and disabilities. And one reason why there are so many resources available is because it's a broad topic. The umbrella descriptor "special needs" can include a child with ADHD and a child with severe autism, a child who has spina bifida and or a child with Down syndrome. And each of these special needs requires different kinds of knowledge and training in order to properly address them. For those of us who minister with children, extending radical hospitality necessitates that we figure out how children with special needs who are in our midst can be full participants in the life of our ministry—and the life of the wider congregation. This is an ongoing journey, because as new children and families come into our churches and ministries, modifications will have to be made to be hospitable if any of these children have special needs.

There's no one correct way of welcoming children with special needs. Each case will be unique and will raise particular issues and challenges that need to be addressed. So perhaps a good first step is to talk with the child's family to get to know the child, and then figure out how to best help the child to participate in your church and your ministries as fully as possible. We are certainly not experts on this, but we offer two examples.

At one church where Ivy served, there was a second grade boy with Asperger Syndrome that manifested itself socially. He had difficulty making friends and certainly didn't want to do anything involving standing in front of people. It was a custom at this church to give Bibles to the second graders and the congregation liked to make a big deal out of it during the worship service. Each child would be invited up front individually to be blessed with a Scripture verse. Then the child would walk over to the minister to receive a Bible to call their own.

Ivy and her team wanted this little boy to participate in this rite of passage, but on some days he wanted to participate in group and social settings, and others he didn't. So she sat down with his mother and worked out a plan. During the ceremony, as it was getting closer to his turn, Ivy was to glance over at his family to get a signal from his mother about whether or not it was a "go." If this boy didn't feel like he could go to the front, his mother would shake her head and Ivy would simply skip over his name. But even if she nodded, there would still be a split second when he might balk at coming forward. That would have been difficult for him and his family.

When the big day arrived and Ivy was reading the children's names, she looked over and his mom nodded. She called his name and held her breath to see what would happen. The young boy got out of his seat and came forward to receive his Bible. His mother was crying. Ivy was crying. It was an incredibly special moment, and everyone—Ivy, the boy, his family and the congregation—was so glad that they had gone the extra mile of contingency plans so this boy could participate in this important congregational milestone.

At another church where Ivy served as children's pastor, two women who had left their jobs as special needs teachers to be stay-at-home parents started a special needs group for those children who, due to more severe disabilities, weren't able to participate in other children's classes or groups. They recruited volunteers to help them, and many people in the church got to know these children because one of their favorite Sunday morning activities was taking long walks around the church building and visiting with the people they met on the way. They adapted practices at this church and created new practices that were conducive and meaningful to the needs of these children. And although they were not able to participate in every aspect of children's ministry, these teachers helped ensure that their young friends could engage in the life of the congregation in meaningful ways. And in the process radical hospitality was extended.

CULTURE

Children today live in a pluralistic society. Mass migration and international travel are relatively easy and inexpensive, and the world has become increasingly culturally diverse. And many faith communities are now marked by cultural diversity as well. The children that are involved in our ministries might not be from our part of the world, and our first language may be their second (or third or fourth).

While churches and children's ministry are becoming more culturally diverse, more colorful and more mosaic-like, cultural diversity continues to be an overlooked topic in discussions of ministry with children. Dave recently spoke at a children's spirituality conference on the topic of cultural diversity, and many of the folks who attended his workshop told him that they'd never heard someone think so intentionally about how cultural diversity shapes (and ought to shape) their work with kids. For many churches people of different cultures are certainly welcome to attend worship, to get involved in congregational life and to share their gifts with the community. But often those who have traditionally held power and control of the church continue to maintain it. In many cases, welcoming cultural "others" means inviting "them" to come and do things "our" way. As one character is the 1988 comedy *Big Business* says, "You're in America now. Speak American."[2]

But this type of attitude isn't sufficient for children's ministry in the way of Jesus. We need to recognize that everything we do in children's ministry is culturally conditioned. The stories we tell, the lessons we prepare, the food we share together at snack time, the music we enjoy, even the way our ministry spaces are arranged come out of cultural assumptions. And the reality is that not all the children in our ministries share these assumptions. We shouldn't expect children who are part of other cultures to fit in and conform to "how we do things here." When we see "our" cultural ways of practicing Christianity and passing on the faith to children as the correct or best ways, it's easy to assume that other people need to learn to do things our way.

There are many culturally conditioned ideas of what it means to follow Jesus. There are several ways to pass on faith to children. Instead of pushing away all that seems "foreign" to us, we can, with the children in our midst, develop a posture of curiosity and, better yet, gratitude for God's gift of cultural diversity. As we reshape how we do ministry with children in order help children with special needs fully participate, we can do the same for children from other cultures. We can explore together ways that Christians of different cultures read the Bible, sing songs to God, share communion and work for justice. As our world continues to become more culturally diverse, the need for children's ministry that addresses and embraces this diversity is going to become more apparent.

KEEPING DIVERSITY DIVERSE

All this goes to show that difference comes in many forms—and so should hospitality. There's a diversity of diversity in the world and in our faith communities. The categories that we include in this chapter are just some of the many forms of diversity in our world. There's no way to adequately address how to offer hospitality to children while keeping in mind every difference that they might bring to congregations.

Christian educator Karen Tye reminds us that "Each human being is complex and multidimensional, and we are called to pay attention to this if we hope to educate in meaningful ways."[3] Each child is a unique individual, and we need to remember this as we seek to nurture these individuals within communities of faith.

Sometimes when we get to know other people, when we learn about them and see them through one of the many lenses for understanding differences among human beings, we may have a tendency to focus on the labels we apply to one another instead of the persons that they are. But each child in our midst is incredibly more complex than the labels we apply to them. Sure, children of one culture seem to act differently than children of another culture. And children who learn visually tend to find some activities more appealing than those who learn kinesthetically. But when we focus too much on the labels we apply to children, we can miss the uniqueness of each child, instead boiling them down to one or two ways that a particular theory or category tells us to see them.

The reason we write about these theories and these ways of understanding diversity is because they remind us that children don't come from a cookie cutter. They remind us of how each one of us is influenced by our socially accepted norms and personal biases. People tend to teach for children who share their learning style and intelligence. People often plan programs and activities without considering how children with special needs might be excluded due to something as simple as not being able to walk down the stairs to a Sunday school room.

For example, as an author and public lecturer, it's a safe bet that Ivy has a dominant verbal-linguistic intelligence. The products resulting from her processing of information are largely written and spoken. Therefore, this is what she is comfortable with as she plans children's ministry activities. But she knows that she needs to move beyond her understanding of how information should be processed, and appreciate all the ways that children are intelligent. The curriculum she currently uses in her church has a component in which children are asked to look at a print of a painting and relate what they see to a Bible story. Because Ivy isn't a visual learner, she never uses these pictures— but she should.

Anytime there is difference, there are power dynamics at work to shape a situation. It's crucial for the sake of our children and for the faithfulness of our faith communities that we recognize this. When people come together across differences, some will tend to hold more power than others. Whatever differences might be present in a community, they tend to stack the deck in favor of one group rather than another.

So being aware of diversity doesn't mean that we should merely start including children who might not have power because of particular differences, that we should simply be open to having "them" join "us." Radical hospitality means that we work to balance the power in a group and this may very well mean that children and leaders alike who have traditionally held power for one reason or another make sacrifices so others can gain power. We need to examine ourselves, our faith communities and our children's ministries to see who has power and who doesn't so we can work to empower everyone, to give everyone a voice and say.

RADICAL HOSPITALITY WHEN DIVERSITY IS ABSENT

Throughout this chapter we've written about hospitality from an assumption that churches and ministry with children are characterized by diversity. In part, we've done this because it represents some of the faith communities of which we've been involved in recent years. And we've also done this because the world we live in is becoming increasingly diverse—and people are becoming more aware of diversity that has always existed in our towns, cities and societies.

But the hard truth is that churches aren't always places of diversity. In fact, as almost every other aspect of our lives becomes more heterogeneous, churches can become bastions where people can find refuge in homogeneity. As Martin Luther King Jr. once famously said, the most segregated hour in the life of the Christian church in the United States is 11 a.m. on Sunday. While he was specifically addressing racial segregation, his prophetic words ring true for other ways we in the church separate ourselves from one another. We Christians are good at creating walls between ourselves, walls that keep us "safe" from folks who are different from us.

As churches remain fairly homogenous in a world that grows increasingly diverse, what implicit messages are we offering to children? Surely young people will notice and feel this dissonance when school, the playground, the shopping mall and even their own families are marked by diversity, a diversity that fades away as they enter their church. As young theologians this disparity can tell them something about the kingdom of God and what it means to follow Jesus. It can tell them that church ought to be a place of refuge from the onslaught of diversity. It can tell them that following Jesus is only for people who look, act, talk and live like "us."

But these messages aren't what Jesus passed on to his disciples through his teaching and his life. Jesus tore down walls that separated people from one another. He pulled together a band of misfits wherever he went. He crossed borders and boundaries in an effort to offer love, compassion and radical hospitality to those who needed it most. Whether eating with tax collectors, asking a Samaritan woman for a drink or telling a parable about a man who crossed cultural lines in order to help a stranger, Jesus' ministry was one of welcoming others with open arms rather than erecting walls to keep them out.

Children's ministry that nurtures disciples of Jesus, then, needs to embody his boundary-breaking acts. We need to take concrete steps in order to extend radical hospitality to all people, not only for the sake of hospitality but also for the sake of modeling the radical diversity of God's kingdom. Nurturing children in the way of Jesus means flinging wide our doors (literally and metaphorically) in order to show children that God's love is for everybody. But we can go one step further and move outside of the church in order to build relationships with people in our towns and cities who are different than we are—not to convert or convince, but simply to befriend.

However, sometimes despite our best efforts and for reasons beyond our control, our ministry with children and our wider faith community can remain fairly homogenous. Perhaps the church has a long history of segregation in the community, and building relationships across lines of difference will take a great deal of patience and time. Perhaps the homogeneity of a church is simply a microcosm of the town or village. Perhaps the worship style of a congregation tends to appeal to a certain type of person. Whatever the case, homogeneity doesn't mean that we're off the hook in offering hospitality. Diversity is always present, even if it's hard to see. It becomes the responsibility of the faith community and its ministry with children, then, to address issues of diversity and homogeneity with children at times and ages when it's appropriate to do so. Perhaps this can be done through excursions to urban centers or by church exchanges, whereby children in churches marked by different types of homogeneity visit one another's congregations. Perhaps it necessitates explicit teaching on the radical hospitality of Jesus and how children can live into God's boundary-breaking story when boundaries that need breaking remain unclear and hazy.

RADICALLY HOSPITABLE CHILDREN'S MINISTRY

Children who are smart in all sorts of different ways, who come from different cultures, whose families come in all shapes and sizes, who have different abilities and disabilities will come into our ministries. Thus, it's important to remember to extend God's hand of hospitality to all children and appreciate what they have to share with us through all the various elements that make up each child. Churches can work to create places where all children, in the dynamic fullness of their entire lives, with all the diversity that they share with us, can participate together in meaningful ways. These churches can become places of radical hospitality, which self-described misfit Letty Russell defined as "the practice of God's welcome by reaching across difference to participate in God's actions bringing justice and healing to our world in crisis."[4]

In *God's Big Table*, Elizabeth Caldwell reminds us that radical hospitality brings with it blessings to all those who experience it. "When all are welcomed into our places of worship, education, and mission, all are blessed."[5] Diversity in all its forms is a gift that God has planted deep into the world. When we see diversity as a blessing and a gift—one that carries challenges with it—we see the world from God's view. And when we minister with children in light of this blessing, we turn our churches and our ministries with children into places of radical hospitality.

At their best, churches ought to be communities where misfits can find a home. They're places where those who feel excluded in other parts of life can find a place of belonging. They're places where God's radical hospitality is extended to those who feel like they don't fit elsewhere. Why should it be any different in ministry with children?

QUESTIONS FOR CONSIDERATION

1. Which practices, customs or liturgies at your church tend to offer hospitality to all children? Which ones may be inhospitable to some children?

2. Does your church ever separate children by age, gender, preference or ability? What messages does this separation or inclusion offer children?

3. How might you find out if any children in your ministry feel like they don't belong? What can you do to show them that they belong?

4. How does your church model a ministry of hospitality for the children in your midst?

9

Intergenerational Community

No better place exists for the most number of people to learn Christian ways from more experienced members of the culture than intergenerational Christian communities. People of all ages and maturity levels are present, actively carrying on the very essentials of Christianity. In intergenerational communities, children learn from each other, younger children, older children, teens and adults. And adults learn from teens and children as well as older adults. All benefit from each other with a sense of mutuality; in essence, they grow each other up into Christ.

HOLLY CATTERTON ALLEN AND CHRISTINE LAWTON ROSS,
Intergenerational Christian Formation

◫ ◫ ◫

UNTIL A RECENT RELOCATION DAVE ATTENDED a small-to-mid-sized Mennonite church in southwestern Ontario, where his wife served as an associate pastor. This congregation is made up of all sorts of people—infants only a few weeks old and folks in their late nineties, members who revel in watching their grandchildren grow in the same church in which they were raised and families who are new to the congregation and sometimes new to the Mennonite tradition, university students, single parents, immigrants and so many other types of people.

One thing Dave really appreciated about this church is that a fairly significant number of congregants regularly get together for all sorts of activities, including games nights, picnics, talent shows and annual church fun weekends at a local campground. Over the years Dave's been involved in other faith communities that held events like these. But they were usually targeted at a specific demographic of the church's membership. One church had dessert nights for women in the second half of life. Another had a small but active youth group that gathered together quite often. And yet another had coffee houses and "mixers" for young adults.

But what makes the community activities at this particular congregation so meaningful for Dave is that they are geared for anyone and everyone. All sorts of people show up with board games in tow for evenings filled with good food and good fun. And, perhaps most remarkably, once everyone is together, the flow, movement and clustering of people is organic. Children don't just run off with other children. The youth don't congregate in a corner of the church hall. The older adults don't settle into chairs to talk with one another all evening. People of all ages enjoy each other's company.

At one of this congregation's church fun weekends, the generations came together throughout the three-day event. Dave learned a song next to people much older and younger than him while his wife joined a class in which a tween taught all sorts of people how to make origami animals. After chatting with grandparents and middle school students during lunch, Dave joined the "bug hunt," where a member of the faith community led people in looking for insects to feed the reptiles that she brought from a conservation area where she works. At first Dave assumed he might be the only bug hunter who had graduated from junior high. But he was delighted when some retirees in the congregation took up the feeding frenzy challenge with more enthusiasm than some of the children! One particular man became the pied piper of the bug hunt, leading children to places where crickets were plentiful and helping kids roll over stones to find the juiciest bugs.

Whether scavenging for insects or sharing a meal at a games night, the people of this church are fostering intergenerational community. They're creating spaces for relationships to flourish across the generations. These sorts of relationships act as buttresses that help children build a solid faith that can sustain them for a lifetime.

In the last two chapters, we tackled issues that push for an interpersonal approach of spiritual formation. In chapter seven we argued that children need to engage in meaningful participation in communities of practice. They need to rub shoulders and bump elbows with fellow community members as they practice their faith together. In chapter eight we spoke about the importance of making room for all children within our faith communities. We put forward a belief in radical hospitality, in helping each child be an active, engaged and meaningful contributor to the life of our children's ministries and congregations.

This chapter grows out of these two ideas. Building on what we've said so far, we issue a call for churches to foster intergenerational communities. The ideas in the past few chapters aren't mutually exclusive. In fact, when you mix together meaningful participation, radical hospitality and intergenerational community, you create a potent catalyst for generating an ecclesial culture for nurturing children's spiritual formation.

We're not the first people to advocate for intergenerational community. In fact, there seems to be a growing consensus that intergenerational relationships and communities are crucial for the well-being of children (and adults!).

Search Institute has been attempting to map out a blueprint for what fosters healthy development in children and youth. Their efforts have led them to identify forty "developmental assets," which they define as "common sense, positive experiences and qualities that help influence choices young people make and help them become caring, responsible, successful adults."[1]

Search Institute has generated reports about their research that identifies developmental assets for young people in four age groups: early childhood (ages 3-5), grades K-3 (ages 5-9), middle childhood (ages 8-12) and adolescents (ages 12-18). Across the board they found that in every age group a crucial developmental asset is "other adult relationships." Whether a preschooler walking onto the school bus for the first time or a teen about to fly away from the family nest, young people benefit from relationships with nonparent adults, with older friends, mentors, teachers, youth leaders and other adults who walk with them on the journey that is life.

In fact, Search Institute found that what really makes a difference in a young person's life is not just whether a person receives support from nonparent adults, but the number of nonparent adults that support them. According to Search, three is the magic number. Receiving support, encouragement and guidance from three or more nonparent adults is a key developmental asset. Through intergenerational community, children and youth have opportunities to form these types of relationships.

The importance of intergenerational relationships is also underscored by Christian Smith's research into the religious and spiritual lives of teenagers in the United States. He spearheaded the National Study of Youth and Religion and reported his groundbreaking findings in the 2005 book *Soul Searching*. Though almost a decade old now, these findings are still one of the best resources we have for understanding the state of young people and religion in the United States.

Smith's astute eye identified a correlation between positive relationships with nonparent adults and adolescent religious commitment.[2] In other words, the more likely a young person was to have supportive nonparent adults in their lives, the more likely it was that this young person would be devoted to her or his particular faith tradition. While we have to be careful not to assume one-way causational relationships (for example, that supportive relationships with nonparent adults lead to religious commitment), we see in Smith's research the importance of intergenerational relationships in the religious and spiritual lives of young people.

To understand one reason why supporting intergenerational relationships matter to the spiritual formation of young people, we turn to Russian psychologist Lev Vygotsky. Writing in the early twentieth century, Vygotsky explored human development and learning in children. He argued that learning happens within a child's zone of proximal development, that is, "the distance between the actual developmental level as determined by independent problem solving and the level of potential development as determined through problem solving under adult guidance or in collaboration with more capable peers."[3]

In other words, children learn best when they engage in an activity that they wouldn't be able to accomplish on their own, but with the help of others they are able to tackle it. Take reading, for example. Young children who are learning the sounds of letters wouldn't be able to sit down and read *Goodnight Moon* or *Hop on Pop* by themselves. But as a parent, babysitter or older sibling helps them sound out each letter and syllable, they are able to pronounce each word and gradually learn to read.

While often used to understand cognitive development, Vygotsky's zone of proximal development is a helpful way of understanding the social nature of spiritual formation and discipleship. As children engage in tasks and activities with people who are older than them, their learning is enhanced and their formation is spurred forward. Again, this is another case that urges us toward intergenerational community. The relationships that children develop with people of other generations allow them to learn within the zone of proximal development and to pass on what they've learned to younger and less-experienced peers.

All this goes to show the importance of fostering intergenerational community as a means for nurturing the spiritual lives of children (and people of other ages too!). Although it's not a new idea, it's often swept under the rug of the lives of faith communities.

But some churches are starting to pull up the carpets. In their recent research into children within "new forms of church," Scottie May and her team found that several of them intentionally emphasize the importance of intergenerational community.[4] In particular, smaller churches tend to be at the forefront of these efforts while age-segregation continues to be the norm in most large congregations.

When we reflect on some of the theological views of community that guide these sorts of churches, it's not surprising to see that some of them are making an effort to become communities where all generations gather together. Churches seeking to rethink and expand what it means to live as disciples today often emphasize a relational ecclesiology or a theology of the church that's built on relationships instead of organizational structure. Many view the faith community like a family and make significant changes to institutional practices in order to ensure that all who are part of this family (regardless of age) are supported as valued members.[5] When coupled with a radical view of hospitality to the stranger, fostering intergenerational community is a way of working to ensure that those who are seen as "strangers among us"—like children—always have a seat at the table.

So intergenerational community not only represents the ideals of Christianity. It's a generative practice that is shaping and reshaping the ecclesial culture of all sorts of churches, including their ministries with children.

But, sadly, many congregations continue to place lines of division among the generations. A quick look at common pastoral titles demonstrates that congregational life continues to be a place where the generations go it alone. Church staff rosters often include a children's pastor, youth minister, pastor to adults, director of young adult ministries and sometimes even a pastor to seniors. Clearly, age-segregation has been the way to go.

Sometimes churches try to kick this habit through family ministry, which is often an attempt to nurture all members of families. But family ministry can easily become children's ministry with adults sitting in, and it can leave single persons, couples without children, empty-nesters and seniors on the sidelines.[6] We dream of intergenerational community that embodies family ministry at its best—ministry with the whole family of God! We dream of children's ministry that benefits from the context of a church joined together rather than segregated by age.

Sometimes congregations might have people of different ages gather in the same space for special events. But even then, it can't be assumed that proximity actually leads to supportive intergenerational community. Having children, youth and adults in the same room at the same time is a very different reality than the image of intergenerational community that we envision. The kind of intergenerational community we imagine is one in which children are spiritually formed through relationships that span the generations and adults receive spiritual renewal from the young people in their congregation who they get to know in meaningful ways. It is a community that shares its common life no matter how young or old a person might be.

NURTURING INTERGENERATIONAL COMMUNITY

Now that we've addressed the importance of intentionally fostering intergenerational community, we'll offer a few practices that we and others have found helpful in this cause. There are, of course, countless creative ways to nurture relationships across generations and spiritually form children in light of these relationships. Holly Allen describes six forms of activities that seem to be promising for forming intergenerational community: including children in worship, special programs or rituals (baptisms, induction of new members, etc.), intergenerational events, family camps, intergenerational Sunday schools or Bible study, and intergenerational small groups.[7] And within each of these broad categories there exist a myriad of possibilities. What we offer, then, are simply three ideas to get the ball rolling in thinking about how we can nurture intergenerational community.

Intergenerational involvement in congregational life. Think of all the simple yet meaningful ways that people contribute to and participate in worship services: song leading, Scripture reading, collecting the offering, distributing Communion, playing musical instruments, sharing stories, reading poetry or prayers, preparing dramatic performances, performing liturgical dances, leading times of reflection or contemplation, and so much more. Children, youth and adults of all ages can join across the generations as they engage in these practices.

This is exactly what happens at Dave's former church that we described earlier in this chapter. It's not unusual to have a child and an adult join together in leading music—with one playing piano and another guiding the congregation in singing. And when it comes to reading Scripture, intergenerational community happens as an older adult and a tween read a psalm in a call-and-response fashion. At times like these, community is formed between the young and old to rehearse songs and figure out how they'll read Scripture together. Although this congregation can do more to reimagine church through intergenerational lenses, these mixed-age leadership teams demonstrate to the entire community that positive mutual relationships are valued within this particular congregation and that children matter to the wider community. And, as we mentioned in chapter seven, intergenerational participation in these and other practices works to apprentice children into the life of a particular community and tradition.

We've had the privilege of visiting and being part of churches filled with creative and innovative people who are transforming the ways that communities of Christ followers worship together. We know several people who have found inspiration for creating new forms of worship in Pete Rollins' book *How (Not) to Speak of God*. As a member of the Irish community Ikon, Rollins has experimented with postmodern forms of worship—many of which don't seem to resemble anything in traditional worship services. But his innovative practices have taken root and led countless leaders and laypeople to play with new kinds of Christian worship. In fact, we believe that many of the worship experiences that Rollins describes are wonderful blueprints (with some adaptation) for intergenerational worship. It is this kind of creativity that's needed to make worship meaningful across the generations. So armed with a spirit of creativity and a willingness to experiment, faith communities can develop all sorts of practices in which the young and old can join together in worship, practices that nurture the spiritual lives of children—and of people of all ages.

And congregational worship—in whatever creative form it might take—is only one small piece of community life. So many opportunities for inviting the generations to come together abound!

A prescription for long-lasting mentorship. In chapter seven we addressed the need for congregations to apprentice young people through guided participation with more experienced members. This can happen spontaneously, as when the older adult at Dave's church started leading children in hunting for insects (although it's safe to say that bug hunting isn't a core or defining practice of this church's life). But it can also happen in more intentional and ongoing mentorship relationships.

We can both think of several people in our lives who acted as mentors to us as we were growing up. Since Dave grew up far away from all his grandparents, aunts, uncles and cousins, a family in the area became his surrogate extended family. Everyone in this family was older than he was, so they all acted as mentors in different ways. Sometimes they taught him about camping—how to canoe and build a decent campfire. At other times they helped him discern where he'd go to university and how he could make use of his gifts and talents in a future vocation. And sometimes they acted as spiritual mentors too. The youngest son in the family, Michael (who was six years older than Dave) was his confirmation sponsor, and Michael's father was always willing to talk about matters related to God, the church and faith.

We're certainly not the only people who had (and continue to have) more experienced mentors who support and challenge us on our ongoing spiritual journeys. The research of Christian Smith, which we discussed earlier in this chapter, shows that many young people have benefitted from relationships with nonparent adults. Mentoring connects neophytes with more seasoned followers of Jesus in order to provide them with meaningful friendships with nonparent adults. At their best, mentors honestly and humbly offer guidance to young people as they walk together on the spiritual journey. At their best, mentors commit to being part of a young person's faith life, celebrating faith (and other) milestones with them and offering safe places to continually wrestle with difficult questions and serious doubts.

We've been involved in churches that have experimented with mentorship initiatives in different ways. In some churches the pastoral leaders that oversee children's and youth ministry seek out adults who are interested in acting as mentors for a particular amount of time and pair these adult mentors with children and youth. In some of these cases lifelong mentoring relationships are formed. When Dave's wife started working as a pastor, she was charged with maintaining a mentorship program that paired youth and adults for the duration of the year. Wanting to get a sense of how the program was run in the past, she approached a few mentors from past lists so she could learn from their experiences. When she asked one older gentleman about his time as a mentor, he said that he's been a mentor to the same young man for several decades. A twelve-month mentoring relationship evolved into an intergenerational lifelong friendship through which the young man (who's not so young anymore) continues to be formed.

Sadly, however, the uniqueness of this story poses a problem. For every long-lasting mentoring relationship that begins from organized mentorship initiatives, there are hundreds that never go beyond the official length of time — if they even last until the designated end date. In many cases the mentor-mentee relationship doesn't bloom. It may grow for a time, but it can wither away for any number of reasons. Perhaps the mentor wasn't terribly committed to walking alongside a young person on the spiritual journey. Perhaps one person experienced a change (in job, school, location, etc.) that brought the relationship to a halt. Maybe the mentor and mentee just didn't mesh well. One pastor recently recounted a meeting she had with the father of a teenager in her congregation. This parent echoed his daughter's experience with the organized mentorship program. His child believes that it puts a label on the relationship and makes his daughter nervous because she feels as though there is significant pressure for her to have an exceptional relationship with the mentor she was assigned.

While there's no way to guarantee that a mentor-mentee relationship will make a significant impact and last for many years, it can help to allow these relationships to form organically. In a church where intergenerational community is a regular part of congregational life, relationships across generations can start to form through everyday interactions. Children and youth can naturally and organically get to know different adults, and adults of all ages can get to know young people. Perhaps at some point, children and youth can be encouraged to name a few people that they might like to have as formal mentors in their lives. Since these relationships would have blossomed without genetic-enhancing efforts of preordained pairings, there's a better chance that these friendships can grow and make a positive impact in the lives of the mentors and mentees.

Mentor-mentee relationships that develop organically speak to a profound shift happening in countless congregations in North America and around the world. It's a shift that Joseph Myers names as one from community that happens through programming and "master plans" to community that develops organically in environments that nurture relationships.[8] When it comes to intergenerational community, this shift can do much to foster relationships of support, encouragement, apprenticeship and mentorship among young people and more experienced members of the faith community.

In an opening monologue for a particular *Seinfeld* episode, Jerry Seinfeld's standup routine is about a trip to a drug store to purchase cold medication. He talks about finding himself before a wall of options, figuring out which one is right for him. One medication is quick-acting. Another is long-lasting. "When do I need to feel good," he says, "now or later?"

This humorous monologue speaks to the difference between assigning young people mentors and allowing relationships to develop organically. It can be fairly simple and quick to pair up adult mentors with young people. But the effects of these quick-acting relationships may soon wear off. Allowing intergenerational mentoring relationships to form naturally can take more time than simply assigning young people with designated mentors. But the fact that a mentor and a mentee choose one another means that this relationship can have a better chance to grow into a long-lasting, meaningful, generative friendship between a young person and an adult willing to walk with them on the spiritual journey. And in the process, mentors can in turn be discipled and positively influenced by their friendships with young pilgrims.

Quick-acting or long-lasting? In the case of mentorship, long-lasting may be the way to go.

Multi-age Sunday school. When it comes to elements of church life that tend to segregate the generations from one another, Sunday school may be the champion. In countless churches it's common for people of separate ages to meet in separate classrooms for separate Sunday school lessons. The adults, young adults, teenagers, tweens and children are split from one another to attend Sunday school classes targeted at people of a certain age. And when it comes to the children, larger churches sometimes break down their classes into children of specific ages. Children's Sunday school classrooms can resemble elementary school classrooms, with kids all born in the same year in the same class. Clearly, Sunday school doesn't seem to be an obvious choice for forming intergenerational community.

But it shouldn't be discounted just yet. We know of one church that has intentionally worked to make Sunday school a place where the generations come together. This church formed Sunday school classes that were made up of seniors, middle-aged adults, emerging adults, adolescents and even older children. And they experienced great success in building relationships across generations and engaging in spiritual formation across the lifespan.

This can seem like a fairly simple practice—get people of different ages together and then do Sunday school however it's already being done. Unfortunately, it's not quite that simple. Adults tend to automatically hold power in multi-age settings, and children and teenagers can be intimidated learning alongside people who are much older than they are. Especially considering how children tend to sit in school classrooms alongside people who are all the same age as they are, it can be daunting to be treated as an equal colearner with people who have years and decades on them.

So when this particular church started experimenting with multi-age Sunday school, they found that some attention needed to be given to the people who would be part of this classroom. They started by recruiting adults who understood and supported the rationale of the initiative and who were sensitive to the young people in the classroom. When they started meeting together, these adults knew that they had to be careful not to dominate conversations, laugh at or dismiss ideas and questions posed by children and youth, and make comments that could be offensive to the young people who were feeling vulnerable about being in the same class as folks who were old enough to be their parents or grandparents—or their parents' grandparents. In this way a gradual rapport and spirit of colearning emerged within this multi-age Sunday school.

Joyce Mercer's research into the spiritual lives of adolescent girls found that many young women long for adult conversation partners. She discovered that girls "wanted mothers, fathers, and other adults in their lives to think critically with them about faith questions. They wanted to push—and have someone respectfully push back. They wanted to be able to ask 'big questions' and search for meaning in the company of adults as well as in the company of their peers."[9] And this longing for adult conversation partners is certainly not unique to the spiritual lives of adolescent girls. Male and female older children, tweens and teens can all be supported and respectfully challenged on the spiritual journey by meaningful conversations with adults in multi-age Sunday school classes.

And while a goal of multi-age Sunday school is to engage young people in spiritual formation through learning from the experiences and wisdom of those who have been around longer than they have, adults within these classes can find themselves inspired, intrigued and challenged by the children and youth. The adults in the church that experimented with this way of doing Sunday school found that they had to get back to basics and revisit theological ideas that they had been taking for granted for much of their lives. And the questions that came from the curious minds of older children and adolescents meant that they couldn't skate around difficult questions. In the end this model of Sunday school proved to be valuable for people of all ages.

BETTER TOGETHER

Since singer-songwriter Bryan Moyer Suderman began recording music over ten years ago, his mission has been simple: "to build up the body of Christ by creating and sharing songs of faith for small and tall."[10] This last phrase—"small and tall"—is what makes his efforts particularly unique. Bryan seeks to unite the church across generations with songs that are meaningful and fun for people of all ages.

But over the past decade or so, Bryan has often been pegged as a children's singer. Although he's consistently said that his music is for "small and tall" alike, countless people erroneously assume that his primary audience is children. His dreams for music that crosses (and tears down) generational borders is challenging to the status quo of generational segregation. In our age-segregated society it's easy for people to assume that anyone who writes songs that children enjoy (but lots of youth and adults enjoy as well) must be a children's singer. Bryan puts in a lot of effort to get people to think otherwise.

This isn't just the case for music. In many facets of society marketers have taught us that the generations should be split up, that some forms of entertainment are meant for children and others are meant for adults. So the word intergenerational is often used to describe something that's intended primarily for children, but which adults can join if they so choose. But *intergenerational* doesn't speak of an adult willingness to "lower" him- or herself and do things meant for children. It means doing community together. It means ensuring that all generations are able to participate together.

At its best intergenerational is simply that—it speaks of all generations, of everyone coming together and mixing things up so that all can be together. It means that children, adolescents and adults of all ages are all present and valued for who they are. So while this chapter certainly belongs in a book about children's ministry, it ought to be a vital topic for books about all kinds of ministry. After all, intergenerational community doesn't just benefit children. Middle-age adults, teenagers, emerging adults and seniors can all benefit from the countless ways that generations can come together as one community.

And as we said about meaningful participation in chapter seven, intergenerational community is a difficult task. Not only does it swim against the tide of society, but it involves bringing together groups of people who see the world differently. After all, *generation* is a word that denotes a demographic of people who were born within a particular span of time and, by virtue of this, have similar attitudes, assumptions, ideas and problems that shape them. A person who came of age during the great depression or WWII will have developed eyes to see and makes sense of the world differently than someone whose childhood and adolescence were defined by the events of September 11, 2001, and the military conflicts over the past decade. A person who grew up during the civil rights movements in the 1960s will have different perspectives and assumptions than someone growing up with the effects of the recent economic downturn.

So, much like fostering interfaith or intercultural community, bringing different generations together means that we're meeting across worldviews as each generation brings its particular if dynamically varied way of seeing the world tucked under its arm. And like any community that forms across lines of difference, intergenerational communities require a continual willingness to move beyond ideas about "us" and "them," whether the "us" is old and the "them" is young or the other way around. It's a tough job, but it honors the spiritual nature of all human beings, the divine spark in the young and the old alike, and Jesus' call to break down boundaries as we seek to uncover God's reign in the world.

QUESTIONS FOR CONSIDERATION

1. Were there any intergenerational relationships or communities that were vital in your spiritual formation as a child? What was it about them that made them so formative?

2. In what aspects of your church's life do the generations come together?

3. How can you work toward developing multi-age Sunday school in your congregation?

4. What are the roadblocks in your congregation toward participation in intergenerational events and education?

10

Transformative Justice

There are young people who I see that want to do something in the world that is meaningful for someone else. Something that is bigger than themselves, and I am convinced that if we lose a generation of young people in the church, it won't be because we didn't entertain them, but because we didn't dare them to do something meaningful with the gospel in light of the world that we live in.

SHANE CLAIBORNE, "Becoming the Church We Dream Of"

◧ ◧ ◧

WE'VE HEARD SOME FOLKS SAY that if you were to remove all the references in the Bible about caring for the poor, the stranger, the other, the oppressed and the indigent, if you removed all the references to the necessity of practiced justice by the people of God, then there wouldn't be much left in the Bible. Old Testament law is a reflection of what God values in respect to the treatment of others and creation. Jesus is a living reflection of God's values of justice and the living embodiment of life in God's kingdom. Since lived and practiced justice is such a significant and crucial part of the message of the Bible, of God's living story, it would seem that any kind of ministry with children would include helping kids understand and practice what it means to work for justice and peace, to help those who are less fortunate, and to live in reconciled relationships with all people and with all creation.

We first wrote this chapter during the beginning and burgeoning of the Occupy movement. And we speak from our particular national contexts.

Ivy lives in the United States, a country devastated by an economic recession where the gap between those who have and those who have not keeps getting wider. And she lives in a time when pressure to shrink the government safety net is getting stronger and stronger. She lives in a country where people increasingly are falling into poverty, and a greater world that is in even more economic distress.

Dave lives in Canada, a nation that, although at times admired for its commitment to the welfare of its citizens, seems to be moving farther away from justice and equality. In recent years the federal government has cut funding to organizations that work for social justice, dismantled emergency healthcare for refugees, ignored the welfare of indigenous peoples and poured copious amounts of money into national defense.

Recognizing that we can no longer be silent about global crises and local injustices, a new generation of Christians is taking a stand. They are learning to walk in the way of peace, justice, compassion and love that Jesus showed. Books, websites, conferences and several other resources are being created to foster versions of Christianity that takes seriously Jesus' call to love your neighbor and yourself. Many Christians are coming to affirm that the heart of the Christian faith is not the church, getting to heaven or even having a personal relationship and connection with God. While these things (and others) certainly matter to the Christian faith, "The main point is God's saving love for creation, God's faithfulness to all of creation, God's ongoing mission of healing a world torn by human injustice so that it can fulfill God's original dream. It is about God's kingdom coming to earth, and it is about God's will being done on earth as it is in heaven."[1]

But how do we teach young people about this? How do we nurture a spirit of justice-seeking in children? What should we be sharing with them about this based on the perspective of God's story?

The topic of children's spiritual formation in light of God's justice is so vast that it deserves to have whole books dedicated to it. So there's no way we can cover everything about educating children to be justice seekers, about what God's story tells us about justice and about children who have made a difference in the world. So for our purposes in this chapter, we'll focus on three overlapping yet distinct ideas or themes: practicing generosity, addressing "isms" (racism, ageism, ethnocentricism, etc.), and making lifestyle choices that reflect justice.

PRACTICING GENEROSITY

We'll admit it. We both have a problem with generosity. And we know where it comes from. It comes from fear. We fear that if we give away money, we won't have enough for ourselves, for emergencies, for unexpected things that might come up—and, to be honest, we also fear that we won't have enough money to go out to dinner, catch a movie or buy a new book when we want to do so. When we were younger, we figured that we'd be generous when we were older and had more money in the bank. But the truth is that we could have $30 million stashed away and we'd still fear that we don't have enough to feel safe and secure if anything should happen to us. However, even though we struggle to be generous, that doesn't mean that we don't try to practice generosity. We do. And even though we've seen God take care of us, we still struggle with fear, anxiety and self-interest whenever we give money away. And even though we both get a wonderful feeling whenever we help others, we still find generosity difficult.

We're sure that we aren't the only people who struggle with generosity because of fear and self-interest. We live in a world where self-interest rules. Everything from our political processes to our church congregational meetings is fueled by each participant's self-interest. So when people do generous things for others, when they act against this tidal wave of self-interest and fear of not having enough, it becomes newsworthy. During the Advent season of 2011, several people were anonymously paying off the layaway bills of others. Both local and cable news stations picked up this story and for a few days it was the go-to feel-good story.

But imagine a world where acts of generosity aren't newsworthy—where they're common, everyday occurrences. Jesus had imagination to see the world this way. And those of us who are parents and ministers seeking to raise children in the way of Jesus need to figure out ways to help them imagine this kind of world. In writing this, our first instinct is to say "this starts at home." While this is certainly true, there's an assumption that parents are poised to pass on a generous faith to children. But who educates and shapes parents in light of Jesus' message of generosity, peace and justice? The answer to this question is most prominently and regularly the local church. So how do congregations help children and families imagine and live into the kind of world that Jesus imagined?

Ironically, we can begin with ourselves. Those of us who pastor, lead and teach in local churches can take a good look at our personal and collective imaginations. How good are we at imagining the kind of world Jesus taught about where his followers understood that, in the same way God cares for the needs of the lilies and the birds, so will God care for us? How good are we at imagining a world where everyone loves their neighbor as they love themselves? How good are we at imagining a world where the returning prodigal child is given a party rather than shamed for his actions? We can't make something happen if we haven't imagined it first. And we certainly can't model it and pass it on to a child if we haven't seen glimpses of this kind of world and imagined it ourselves.

If we who follow Jesus have trouble imagining this kind of world, maybe it's because we're afraid. Sometimes it seems like Christians, people who profess to love God and live in the way of Jesus, are the most fearful people we know. We're afraid that if we give our money away we won't have enough for ourselves, even though Jesus tells us this is not the case. We're afraid that there aren't enough hours in the day to do all that we have to do for ourselves and our families, let alone people we don't even know. We're afraid that governments are waging "wars on religion" when God's story is one of infiltrating the world with love rather than with fear and retaliation. And this gets in the way of our ability to imagine and live into the world Jesus lived and died to bring about.

So what does all this have to do with helping kids become generous Christians? Maybe we can teach them a song about giving to others and show them an animated movie about the little boy with five loaves and two fishes. Although this might entertain them, it probably won't go a long way in forming them into generous justice seekers. For both adults and children, true generosity needs to be modeled and true justice-seeking needs to be lived out together. Children learn far more from what they see and do than what they hear. If we're ever to help people overcome their fear of not having enough for themselves, we need to help them start becoming generous and see what a life of generosity looks like when it's lived out in the long term.

Ivy was once privileged to take a class with the esteemed Christian educator John Westerhoff. In this class he spoke about the importance of modeling generosity and justice to children. He lamented the fact that children aren't usually part of congregational worship services when the offering is collected, so they don't have the opportunity to see this even small act of generosity in the faith community. He also mentioned that it's rare to see clergy put anything in the offering plate. They usually sit up front and the ushers don't typically pass the plate to them. Westerhoff suggested that the clergy correct this problem and put something in the offering plate each week as a model to the rest of the congregation.

At Ivy's current church the children gather together for "circle time" before they leave for their Sunday school classes. Part of the ritual of circle time is collecting the offering. Each week, Ivy makes sure to drop something in the offering basket so she's a model of generosity to these children. If parents want to raise children who are generous, they need to be generous themselves and their children need to see this.

When Dave was growing up, he didn't like going to children's liturgy. So he stayed with his parents for the whole of Mass each Sunday. At one point the collecting of the offering came to be one of his favorite parts of the Mass. He enjoyed seeing those who were collecting the offering slowly make their way to where he was sitting with his family. His parents would give him the envelope with his family's offering, and he'd reach out and proudly place it into the basket when it was his turn. When he would ask his parents what this money was used for, they'd tell him about all the projects that their church was involved in. And sometimes the priest asked Dave and his family to collect the offering that week. So not only was he able to see his family give generously, but he got to see all sorts of people reach into their purses and pockets and support the work of this local parish in their community and around the world. By being part of the Sunday offering, Dave learned from his family and the faith community the importance of giving generously.

However, there is more to generosity than dropping some money into a basket. Helping children to have a generosity of spirit is important too—maybe more important. This has to do with how we treat others. Of course, we think it's important to always say please and thank you. We try to let other people into traffic in front of us when we can. And we try to be helpful to strangers in small ways. These are simply some basic examples of generosity of spirit, which involves giving to others in ways that involve more than money and involves more than being polite. It means treating others the way we'd want to be treated through even the smallest and most simple acts of kindness.

And in some ways this is more difficult than making an online donation to a favorite organization. We may agonize over writing a check or giving money away, but once we write the check or press "submit," we don't tend to think about it anymore. But being generous in other ways is not always so cut and dried. It takes more courage to have a generous spirit.

So we need to demonstrate to children more than fiscal generosity. We need to show them what it means to treat others with the dignity, respect and humanity that we'd want to be treated with. Craig Kielburger (who founded Free the Children at only twelve years of age) and his brother Mark learned to have a generous spirit from watching their mother interact with those who society often forgets.

> When some parents come across a homeless person while out with their children, they cross to the other side of the street. Our mother used to stop. Without fail, she would strike up a conversation. It was never more than a few sentences: Was it cold last night? What is your name? Where are you from? Have you been in the city a long time? Sometimes we were impatient, not quite understanding why we couldn't just continue to the mall or wherever else it was we were going. But years later, we understood the lesson. By acknowledging that person's presence and

exchanging those few words, our mother taught us to see the humanity in every person and the value of respecting everyone, no matter who they are.[2]

When Craig and Mark's mother acted out of a generous spirit—through giving her money and, more importantly, treating others as she would want to be treated—she was living in the way of Jesus. And her sons were watching. And the children in our lives are watching us.

So children need to see us having a generous spirit to others. But they also need to be recipients of this spirit. We can't teach them to follow the Golden Rule and then treat them in ways that we (and they) don't want to be treated.

It should be clear by now that we are strong advocates for having every person in the faith community participate in the corporate worship of that community. And barriers to making this happen largely arise from self-interest of clergy and adults in the community and their unwillingness to lend a generosity of spirit to the children and youth in a congregation.

Let's talk about the adults first. We've heard adults refer to their church worship services as "my" worship (as if worship can be commodified and owned). But worship is not about us. It is about God. Some people miss this point and instead search for churches that offer worship services that make them comfortable and meet their standards of aesthetics and predictability. And predictability may be more important than aesthetics. Ivy suspects that for many people daily life has become so stressful and unpredictable that the only predictable part of their lives is the Sunday worship service. So this causes great resistance to any kind of change in the worship service that might be more accommodating to children and youth. Add to that the fact that we live in a world of entertainment, instant gratification and endless commodification, and it's no wonder that worship services are seen as products that need to appeal to our wants and needs.

Clergy can also put up barriers to full participation of every member because they may not want to deal with the resistance of the congregation and they may think sermons have more impact than they really do. There are approximately six hundred thousand ordained Protestant clergy in the United States alone. Do we really think that many people are so talented at public speaking that they are able to deliver a scintillating, life-changing message forty-eight Sundays a year?

There's a connection here. As we said in earlier chapters, congregational worship services aren't usually planned with young people in mind. So when they participate in worship, they're told (explicitly or implicitly) to do it our way. Jeremiah Wright commented on this phenomenon in a presentation for the 2012 Children, Youth, and a New Kind of Christianity conference, saying that we attempt to turn young people into robots, into miniature versions of ourselves, instead of letting their interests, needs and lives transform how we worship God together. It would be a wonderful example of generosity of spirit to our children and youth if our congregations and clergy were willing to step out of their comfort zones and (re)imagine worship that might be both pleasing to God and reflective of all people that make up our faith communities. Isn't this how we adults would want to be treated? Again, it may be our lack of imagination regarding worship that wraps us up in our own self-interest and causes us to withhold generosity from those who need it.

This is simply one example of how we can teach children to have a generosity of spirit by extending this spirit to them. But the possibilities are endless.

REACHING INTO RIVERS

Generosity is part of living into God's story and following Jesus. But Christians are called to go further than generosity. We're called to teach our children to do more than simply give of our money, time and gifts to help people flourish. We're called to change the world with our children.

There's a great little metaphor for illustrating this. Many Christians are like people standing at the edge of a river, reaching in to rescue those who have fallen in, are being pulled down by the undertow and are drowning. We reach out and take hold of those who need a hand and we pull them out until they are safe on the riverbank. But we don't often ask *why* these people are in the river in the first place. We save them from the rapids and the undertow, but we don't try to stop the forces that are pushing them into the river several miles upstream.

One way of describing these forces that throw people in the river is through harmful "isms"—racism, sexism, ageism and so on. These and other damaging isms—unlike those isms that seek to overturn injustice, like womanism, feminism, childism—are sinful ideologies that hold that some people are better than others and that give rise to discriminatory practices of exclusion, oppression, marginalization and injustice. We who follow Jesus, who are trying to practice a type of red letter Christianity in which the words (and actions) of Jesus are taken seriously, need to do more than simply teach children to be generous. We need to teach them to challenge the status quo, to chip away at those isms that threaten human and nonhuman life on our planet, to act justly, love mercy and walk humbly (Mic 6:8).

We believe that ministry with children ought to help them learn about the dangers and sinfulness of damaging isms. As we wrote this chapter the United States was in a heated conversation about the murder of an unarmed young black man in Florida, which brought the subject of racism to the forefront. Also as we wrote the United States was slowly emerging from a deep and disastrous recession. Unemployment was dropping, but not for folks over fifty. Of course, blatant ageism played a role in this. And a 2012 presidential candidate was advocating that women should not find their way into the workplace but instead stay home to live out their roles as wives and mothers.

These examples come from just one country. One can see the harmful results racism, ageism, sexism and other manifestations of oppression and injustice in every context. For example, the leadership of the Attawapiskat First Nation community in northern Ontario, Canada, has declared a state of emergency for the past few years because housing has been inadequate for protecting residents from dropping temperatures as autumn turns to winter. Yet the Canadian government and countless citizens do little to nothing to bring justice in the form of shelter and healthcare to local residents, let alone work to transform unjust ideologies and practices that led to this problem in the first place. Fortunately, the Idle No More movement is bringing a new level of awareness to injustices faced by Aboriginal peoples, but there is still much more that can be done.

The isms are alive and well in our culture, and unfortunately the church can sometimes reflect culture rather than help it imagine a better way. It can be easy to see how other people and institutions perpetuate unjust ideologies. But it's much more difficult to admit to the prejudice and discrimination that exists in our own communities, churches, homes and personal lives.

How can we who minister with young people help them become people who imagine a better way? How can parents, ministers, teachers and leaders nurture a spirit of Christ-centered justice seeking in children that tears down barriers erected by unjust ideologies? We offer a few ideas, knowing that these are just drops in a bucket of possibilities.

First, we need to continually remind our children that God loves everyone. God loves people of all colors, faiths, ages, abilities, genders, sexual orientations, nations and political persuasions. God loves people we may find despicable. Sometimes this is hard to swallow. We imagine that the people who heard Jesus tell the parable of the good Samaritan found the ideas of the hated Samaritan as their neighbor and the hero of the story hard to swallow. But Jesus imagined a world where this was so, a world where enemies become more than friends, a world where they became coconspirators plotting healing in a broken world. Hopefully, we can help our children imagine a world where this is so. And hopefully we can open ourselves to learning from children's ability to imagine worlds of justice, fairness and friendship.

Second, children's ministry can offer young people opportunities to know people who are different from them. Building relationships across lines of difference replaces hostility for "the other" with solidarity with those who are different from oneself. After all, "Christian mission begins with friendship—not utilitarian friendship, the religious version of network marketing—but genuine friendship, friendship that translates love for neighbors in general into knowing, appreciating, liking, and enjoying this or that neighbor in particular."[3]

Ages ago, in seminary, Ivy was researching a paper on moral development. She ran across a small study that was exploring why the Woolworth's department store in Greenwich, Connecticut (then as now one of the wealthiest towns in the United States), had the highest level of teenage shoplifting of any Woolworth store. The people who were shoplifting were upperclass kids who could afford to buy the items they were stealing. The writers of the study compared the shoplifters to other teens who lived in a wealthy suburb in Boston, where apparently the local Woolworth's store didn't experience the same level of theft. The researchers wondered what the difference could be.

A common characteristic of the Boston kids was that many of them attended schools in the city where, at that time, they had to travel by public transportation through diverse neighborhoods to get to school. The Greenwich teens, on a daily basis, only saw other residents of Greenwich, which was and still is a fairly insular and homogenous community. The researchers posited that perhaps a key variable affecting these teen's proclivity toward shoplifting was their exposure to people who were different from them.

Ivy's always found this little study fascinating. Time and again, it leads her to wonder how churches can be places where children encounter difference, where relationships with people who look, speak and act differently are cultivated. But the great majority of churches where we've both served have not been very racially, culturally or economically diverse. Perhaps the partnering of racially or culturally segregated churches around their children and youth ministries might be a way to encourage diversity. Some churches do this partnering with youth and adult ministries, but patterns of racism, prejudice and privilege can already be well established by then and may continue to work in covert ways. It's best to start early, with toddlers, preschoolers and children. Churches that are often separated by lines of difference can begin visiting each other, doing ministry in one another's buildings and neighborhoods—with each other in these spaces—and share ideas and meals with one another. Think of the powerful message this would send to children as these practices of border crossing became "what church is to them" and a normal part of their lives. Think of the powerful witness this would send to the surrounding neighborhood and the greater world about how people living in the way of Jesus can work at transcending fear and smacking prejudice in the face.

Children and youth don't need to leave the church building to build relationships with people who are different. If children fully participate in the faith community (as we argue in chapter seven) and if a church and its ministry with children is radically hospitable (as we argue in chapter eight), then, in theory, children should naturally rub shoulders with people who are different from them, at least by virtue of age. However, churches that are more homogenous might actually need to leave the building in order to build these sorts of relationships—which is something that Jesus has expected of the church all along.

As we've said in chapter nine, in many churches the generations are so successfully separated that children might never know there are older people around, let alone know them by name. We believe that relationships across generations can positively influence the spiritual formation of all those involved. But an added benefit of those relationships is that children grow up knowing people who are several generations removed from them. They grow up knowing what adults have to offer the world at any age. And if children are exposed to emotionally healthy and faithful older disciples, this helps them to escape the current world that worships at the altar of youth, a world that looks down on those who allow themselves to get old. And it helps them imagine with Jesus a world where age does not define worth.

We can also bring children up in faith communities where women are respected and valued, where women's voices are encouraged and heard and their gifts are recognized and affirmed. Children can grow up in communities that stand with women against any kind of domestic violence and who stand with women struggling with poverty and other injustices. Girls can be raised in communities where they will be respected, taught and shown that they can be whoever and do whatever God has gifted them to be. And boys can be raised in communities where they see men who stand as allies with women.

When we create communities like this, communities that help the marginalized, oppressed and poor to work for justice, we show children what it means to be a disciple who lives in God's reign. We demonstrate what it means to become a protagonist in God's story, and we teach them that this story is one of justice, peace and hope for the world.

Of course, this can be challenging work. It's easier to teach children that God loves them than it is to teach them about injustice in the world. It's easier to teach them to obey their parents and share with friends than it is to get into some of the complexities surrounding suffering. We may even feel like we're putting too much on our children by talking about more difficult issues like injustice, violence and poverty. So we do well to pass on to children Pamela Couture's advice to "Start with a small commitment that can be regularly sustained."[4] We can help them work step by step, ensuring that they (and we) don't bite off more that they can chew. Spiritual formation that takes justice seriously is a gradual process that seeks to help children learn how to be justice seekers in age-appropriate ways.

Shane Claiborne has said that "if we lose a generation of young people in the church, it won't be because we didn't entertain them, but because we didn't dare them to do something meaningful with the gospel in light of the world that we live in."[5] When we invite and equip young people to live into God's story of love and reconciliation, we dare them to become protagonists in this story. When we lovingly challenge them to work for justice and peace in the world, to seek first the kingdom, we offer them ways to make their lives meaningful.

HOW THEN SHALL WE LIVE?

Children's ministry is about discipleship. It's about learning to live in the way of Jesus. And one way of understanding what it means to be a disciple is through Jesus' command to love God with all your heart, soul, mind and strength, and to love your neighbor as yourself.

What does this look like? Christian interpretations of this command are incredibly varied and diverse. The purpose of this chapter isn't to define what kind of lifestyle exemplifies what loving God and loving neighbors is all about—it's going to look different in each of our contexts. Instead, our goal in this chapter has been to help readers think about how to engage in discussions and practices of living in the way of Jesus in our ministry with young people. The ways we can help children chip away at injustices will vary according to our particular contexts. So we don't want to attempt to nail down exactly what it means for children to live in the justice-seeking way of Jesus, because context matters. But we believe that young people should be part of conversations about what this means; they should get to know those who are trying to follow Jesus in their own ways; and they should be seen as active justice seekers wherever they may be.

And living as justice seekers with children can begin within our own congregations. We know of one church that packed simple bag lunches that could be kept on hand for when homeless or disadvantaged persons knock on the door and ask for help. Children can get fully involved in each aspect of this practice. They can help decide what people might need and like in these lunches, accompany leaders to the grocery store to purchase food, pack the bags during Sunday school or youth group, and even pass the food out to those who come looking for help. And all along the way leaders can talk with children about social and theological issues surrounding homelessness and poverty so that this simple bag-lunch ministry can eventually lead to other initiatives, like letter-writing campaigns and hunger strikes, that struggle against the root causes of homelessness.

Perhaps children can love their neighbors by getting out of the church and working to clean up their communities and care for the earth that we share with our neighbors around the globe. Ben Lowe is an environmental activist who has worked with refugee and immigrant children in Illinois in order to educate them about creation care by getting down to business and practicing environmental stewardship in their own neighborhood. They tackled a littering problem head-on by plastering the community with signs that discouraged littering and fanning out across the community to clean up the trash and recyclables that were scattered around the neighborhood. He's also spearheaded a community garden that the children in the community helped to build. Although some folks in the neighborhood scoffed at the idea, thinking that the kids would trample the seedlings before they had a chance to grow, the children became the garden's greatest champions. As they picked up trash and tended to their vegetable plants, the children were learning about how to care for the earth and, in the process, care for those around them.

There are countless other ways to help children love their neighbors through how they live. After Hurricane Sandy hit the eastern United States, many people in the New York City area (including Ivy) were looking for ways to help hurricane victims. Ivy wanted the children in her church to be able to contribute to the relief efforts, but most of them were too young to go to the work sites and shelters. So instead she helped these kids assemble hygiene kits full of towels, washcloths, toothbrushes and other necessities of life for people who had lost everything in the hurricane. Ivy's church in Manhattan also enlisted the children and families of their weekday enrichment programs to create craft packets for community centers and schools in the areas hardest hit by the storm. These packets helped these places continue to offer services to children and families even if their supplies had been wiped out, and they gave children who had also lost much or everything a creative outlet and a joyous experience.

Whether packing bag lunches, tending a community garden or making hygiene kits for hurricane victims, children make meaning about following Jesus by rolling up their sleeves and getting their hands dirty. They learn about justice seeking by living in ways that help to repair the world. But what happens when churches keep their doors locked and don't let children get out into the neighborhood because they are afraid that something might happen to their kids? These fears are legitimate. We want our children to be safe. But the truth is that walking in the way of Jesus means taking some risks. Being a disciple means going into the world and entering into situations that others would probably choose to avoid. And this is risky. But it's also risky to bubble wrap children and avoid exposing them to any world that isn't first sprayed with disinfectant. In these cases the risk is one of undermining spiritual formation in the way of Jesus by leaving out the justice seeking that is a fundamental aspect of living as a disciple. This doesn't mean that we should bus all our kids to the most dangerous parts of our cities every weekend, but that we break the bubble wrap and gradually and appropriately help them chip away at injustice wherever they may be.

We who want to help children live as disciples of Jesus can work to show them that they are connected to others, that following Jesus means loving neighbors far and wide. All people are our neighbors.

And this planet is our neighbor. Children's spiritual formation can involve helping young people understand how their lifestyle decisions affect others. We may not be able to solve global crises (or even local injustices) through our discussions and practices, but we can raise the consciousness of children, unnumbing their imaginations so that perhaps younger generations might be able to, with God's help, create lifestyles that truly reflect love of God and neighbor. We can help children see that their voices and actions are valuable assets in the quest for justice.

When we help children enter the story of God, we can't help but encounter Jesus' words about caring for the poor, words about loving God and loving neighbor. When we teach children what it means to follow Jesus, we can nurture connections between God's story and their stories by drawing contrast of God's vision for justice with the unjust world we live in. And in so doing, we work to form disciples who are excited and determined to join God where God is already working to transform the world. And their excitement and determination can in turn rub off on us as we continue to challenge one another to live in the way of Jesus.

QUESTIONS FOR CONSIDERATION

1. In what ways does you church encourage children to practice generosity?

2. How can these practices move from helping children have generous hearts and spirits to helping them address the root causes of injustice?

3. What concrete action can you and the children in your ministry take to model transformative justice to the wider church (advocate for reusable cups for coffee hour, install recycling bins, "trick or treat" for food for a local food bank rather than candy, and so on)?

4. In what ways does your church teach or model for children how to live in reconciled relationships with each other and with the planet we call home?

11

Holistic Lives

Our new paradigm must broaden the context of
Christian education to include every aspect of our individual
and corporate lives within an intentional, covenanting, pilgrim,
radical, counter-cultural, tradition-bearing faith community.

JOHN H. WESTERHOFF III, *Will Our Children Have Faith?*

□ □ □

WHEN DAVE WAS ON STAFF AS a children's pastor at a mid-sized congregation, he was responsible with overseeing programs for children in the neighborhood—summer day camps, evening family events, vacation Bible school and a breakfast club, to name a few. And through this involvement in the community outside his church's doorstep, Dave was able to meet all sorts of families.

One family that he had the privilege of meeting was made up of a thirty-something single mother who was raising three boys between the ages of seven and eleven. Each of these boys lived with a behavioral or developmental disorder. Their mother was a strong and determined woman who was thriving at raising her children against all odds. She would walk these three boys to the summer day camp every morning and talk with Dave as her children helped him get organized for the day. They always wanted to pitch in. And at the end of each day, she'd collect them from the church and take them home and, for a time, this was the extent of Dave's involvement in their lives.

But things changed as Dave got to know them. Over time, he noticed that they had trouble making friends, following instructions and understanding lessons. He learned that this certainly wasn't unique to the programs he ran. They'd been having a tough time with these things at school as well. Dave quickly discovered that these boys needed more from him than simply to have fun and learn about matters of faith. They needed a nonparent adult—particularly a male adult—to care about them. So Dave intentionally got to know this family, these children. He made sure that they always had someone to play with when they were at the church and that they had a caring nonparent adult to talk to about their problems and share their joys. And when their mother was unexpectedly hospitalized for several days, he stopped by their home to shoot hoops with them, play with them at a local playground and make sure that they had someone to talk to during this crisis.

This family taught Dave about the importance of the whole of a child's life. Children's ministry isn't just about one's spiritual life or faith life, as if these things could be separated from the rest of the self. Children's ministry must consider the whole child. It must treat children's lives as holistic. As Doug Pagitt reminds us, "when we minister to people, we minister to the whole person."[1]

So children's ministry should treat children as holistic human beings. In one sense we see children as holistic *human* beings when we affirm that the spiritual life of children is not separate from the rest of their lives, all the aspects of our lives that make us human are bound up with each other. Spiritual formation occurs in conjunction with other aspects of human growth and development. And in another sense we see children as holistic human *beings* when we affirm that the kids who come to church are the same kids who go to school five days a week, who take piano lessons or play on hockey teams, who take care of younger siblings and struggle to get their homework done on time. Spiritual formation can help children follow Jesus in the whole of their lives and *be* Christian wherever they are—not only at church.

HOLISTIC *HUMAN* BEINGS

One of Ivy's most interesting and stimulating professors in graduate school was Ted Ward. Among many fascinating ideas, Ted has an interesting theory about spiritual development—"the hand theory." In his classes Ted would hold up his hand and count off areas of human development on his fingers: physical development, intellectual development, emotional development, social development and moral development. Then he'd say that Christian educators often like to add a sixth finger to the hand: spiritual development. But Ted didn't believe in the six-fingered hand of development. He said, instead, that the spiritual life of the person was found in the palm of the five-fingered hand because all of the other areas of human development have an effect on spiritual formation, and spiritual formation can in turn affect other areas of human growth.

How a person grows, forms and develops in spirituality, in relational consciousness and in the quest to transcend is influenced by how that person develops in all other areas. All of one's life is intertwined and interconnected. We are whole persons. So as we think about the spiritual formation of children, we need to be concerned about and informed in all areas of their development—not just their spiritual capacities.

Physical development. More and more folks are discovering the truth in the old adage "you are what you eat." What we eat affects not only our physical well-being but also our ability to think and our moods, which in turn affect how we relate to others and the world and even the decisions we make. Children who attend school without breakfast don't tend to do as well as those who've had the "most important meal of the day." It seems that every day a new study is released showing a connection between something we eat and it's good or ill effects—not just on our physical body but on our other capacities, like thinking and feeling. So if the well-being of our bodies influences how we think, feel, process information and relate to others, then it makes sense that a child's physical development and condition will affect his or her spiritual development.

However, what seems less clear is how one's spiritual vitality affects one's physical development. For centuries Christians have quoted Paul's words that "your body is a temple of the Holy Spirit" (1 Cor 6:19) as an admonition against certain types of amusements. However, at least in some circles we've been involved in, the prohibitions don't extend to the kinds of foods we put in our bodies. The scriptural prohibition against gluttony is rarely mentioned, even though it's an incredibly important issue in our world today. Yet as we grow in our relationships with God and learn to follow Jesus and love our neighbors, we can become more aware of what that means for how we take care of ourselves. Spiritual formation can begin to consider the body and how we think about food and other substances we put in it.

So it seems appropriate that a part of ministry with children, youth and families can focus on how we take care of our bodies because it is important for our well-being. The health of our bodies can influence how children learn and understand what it means to be a person who loves God and follows Jesus.

Any of us who have children or who have watched the children in our lives grow up have been witnesses to wonders of physical development. Young parents monitor every new physical skill a baby learns to make sure she or he is developing on schedule. We look forward to those first words and first steps. But as many people watch children grow in front of them, fewer think about how physical development can impact a child's spiritual formation.

The development of our brains is part of our physical development. Even though it's responsible for many things, many people tend not to think of it as physical, to consider that it grows with our bodies through childhood just like our legs and arms. And the brain, which is the organ responsible for how we think about, experience and feel about the world, is an important component of spiritual formation and health. Several neuroscientists and neurotheologians are engaging in critical and groundbreaking research about how the brain is hard-wired to have spiritual experiences, connecting physiology and spirituality in intimate ways.[2]

While we'll be among the first to say that how God operates in our lives is ultimately a mystery, we believe that God uses our brains, the center of intellect and emotion. Some people believe that discoveries about how the brain processes spiritual experiences prove that a deity does not exist. But we don't think neurological discoveries about spiritual experiences disprove the existence of God. In fact, we think (along with some neurotheologians and neuroscientists) that such research helps us understand how our brains were created to put us in relationship with God.[3] So how well our brains function can shape how we understand, feel and experience God in our lives. And since brain development is affected by events and experiences during childhood, the brains of the kids in our congregations and families matter to their spiritual development.

The limitations and possibilities of development at certain ages determine what tasks we are able to perform. This matters a great deal to children's spiritual formation. When children are expected to do things they are not yet physically able to do (like asking a two-year-old to sit still on a chair for a long period of time), they can internalize the failure to do as asked and believe it to be their fault that they can't accomplish the task. In reality, the adult in the room shouldn't have expected the child to perform such a task in the first place. When this is done to a child repeatedly, the child can begin to feel unlovable and incompetent. Kids might think that something is wrong with them and they may even fear punishment. Sometimes a child who feels unlovable and incompetent may even find it hard to understand that God loves him or her. So an understanding of age-appropriate expectations in the area of physical development for parents and caregivers of young children is so important. Children's brains, along with the rest of their bodies, matter to the vitality of their spiritual lives.

Intellectual development. Some churches and streams of the Christian faith believe that what a person knows is what really matters, particularly whether the person knows and can articulate that Jesus died on the cross for her or his sins. In many of these contexts, children's ministry becomes a means of helping children understand this theological belief so that they can be counted among the saved.

Such churches and initiatives in children's ministry tend to focus on the intellectual or cognitive development of children. After all, they believe that what a child *knows* is what really matters. And while we disagree with the narrow focus of their formational efforts, we believe that they're absolutely right that children's cognitive development matters!

One's intellectual or cognitive development depends on one's physical development. As our brains develop, we are better able to reason about our world and environment, and we are able to make meaning in different ways. As human beings grow, we develop problem-solving skills and our capacity to synthesize knowledge and experiences grows with our bodies. For children in congregations this knowledge and experience includes information and meaning made about the Bible, church life, God and people who love God and try to live in the way of Jesus.

It's important that we who minister with children guide them in gaining knowledge and making sense of experiences in age-appropriate ways. We can help them put information together and make meaning in ways that enable them to more fully know God, follow Jesus and see the Holy Spirit's work in their lives.

Emotional development. Psychologist Erik Erikson posited that human beings go through several emotional crises between birth and old age that determine their degree of emotional health. If a crisis is not navigated successfully, Erikson held that a person would need to renegotiate a stage later in life.

Erikson believed that a child's first emotional crisis is between trust and mistrust. Optimally, we hope the child will emerge out the other side being more trustful than distrustful. This is more likely to happen when a child has caregivers who are trustworthy and who help that child build appropriate levels of trust.

As children move out of infancy, they move to the stage of autonomy versus shame and doubt. This often occurs during the preschool years, when kids are learning to do things for themselves. In order to emerge successfully (feeling good about learning and using new skills) from this stage, the child needs to be affirmed for attempts at independence and shouldn't be expected to do things that are inappropriate for his or her age and capabilities.

These emotional stages matter for the spiritual formation of children. If we wish for children to form trust in God, they need to see people as trustworthy. When they understand what it means to trust a physically present and tangible human being, they can more fully understand what it means to trust an intangible God.

Furthermore, in order for children to understand and feel that God loves them, they needs to see themselves as lovable and competent. We know countless people who have struggled (and still struggle) to truly believe that God loves them because they have so much trouble finding any worth in themselves. They've come through the second emotional crisis holding onto shame instead of autonomy. The seeds of seeing oneself as lovable and competent are sown in the autonomy-versus-shame crisis. When a child is successful at and appropriately praised for achieving independence through age-appropriate tasks, she begins to understand that she is lovable and competent. When a child is loved and praised by the adults in his life, this helps him to feel as though God loves him too. This is why it is so important for parents and caregivers to be trustworthy, to understand age-appropriate expectations and to appropriately praise children for their successes and encourage them to keep trying when they fail. (Of course, too much praise can go to a child's head and give her or him unrealistic expectations about her or his abilities.)

So the emotional lives of children are interwoven with their spiritual lives. Children who develop in emotionally healthy ways can be predisposed to a healthy spirituality, and those who go through spiritual formation in positive ways will be on the road to emotional health as well.

Social development. Following Jesus was never meant to be an individual, solitary pursuit. Throughout God's story we can read about all sorts of people who banded together in their quest to live according to the will of God and to be disciples of Jesus. The ancient Israelites lived in tribes and clans in which they tried to live by God's words and pass them from one generation to the next. Jesus called together disciples to follow him with each other, to live with one another. And God sent the Holy Spirit to this band of followers as they gathered in community in the Upper Room, which was the beginning of the church, of the faith *community*.

Human beings are communal animals. We survive and thrive when we work together.

So children's social development, how they learn to positively relate to and work with others, matters to their spiritual formation. After all, we showed in chapter two that spirituality is inherently relational. And that's why we've dedicated chapters in this book to addressing participation in communities, creating hospitable spaces and fostering intergenerational relationships. Children develop socially *and* spiritually as they learn to live with others in the community of faith and appreciate the benefits of that community. And the relational skills that kids develop as members of such a defined community can help their appreciation of other social groups and relationships. Being part of a hospitable and radically welcoming community helps them learn to be hospitable to others.

But if a community is closed off, unwelcoming and intolerant of those who are different than they are, this can affect the social development of children who grow up in those circles. How we interact with children, with one another and with those outside of our communities can shape how children learn to interact with people as they seek to be salt and light to the world.

When children find a sense of belonging in a faith community and reap positive benefits from this belonging, they can be poised to see themselves as people who matter, who others enjoy being around, and they may seek to cultivate positive relationships in other circles. When children feel like they belong, like they matter to their community, they are more apt to help others feel this as well.

So social development matters to children's well-being. It's important for faith communities to give the children in their midst opportunities to feel like they belong in the same way they want adults to have a sense of belonging and ownership in the community. They deserve to be greeted at the door, to be involved as doers in ministry and projects, to have opportunities to know all the generations that make up the community, and to be meaningfully involved in the community's worship life. Participation in ritual binds social groups together. Therefore, when children participate in the rituals and practices of their social groups, they can experience a profound sense of belonging to something greater than themselves.

Moral development. While developmental theorist Jean Piaget studied the development of moral awareness in his research into children's cognitive abilities, it was Lawrence Kohlberg who put the study of moral development on the map. He built on Piaget's work to discover how human beings reason about making moral judgments. His hypothesis was that regardless of the context and content of one's morality, how one reasons and acts morally moves through several stages.[4] However, Kohlberg thought that people could get stuck in early stages of moral development and never move beyond them, a predicament likely caused by the types of moral communities and contexts a person belonged to.

Many among those of us who do ministry with children or who raise children in our homes to live in the way of Jesus may hope that there is a strong correlation between being spiritually mature and thinking and acting in ways that our Christian contexts define as ethical or moral. So it's helpful for us to understand that children reason differently about morality, about what is right and wrong, at different stages of their life. As we said in chapter ten, helping children think about issues of justice and injustice ought to be gradual and done in ways that don't expose them to more than they're ready to know. For example, preschoolers tend to think that an action is right or wrong if someone receives punishment for the action. And grade-school-age children will reason that an act is wrong if a respected or feared authority figure tells them so. When we understand this about children we can have appropriate expectations for a child's moral views and understand the true extent of our influence on a child's ability to reason morally.

But, more importantly, as cultivators of a child's spiritual formation, it's important to be concerned about two things that grow out of theories of moral development. First, it behooves us to be aware of our own moral life and ethical beliefs, to have a sense of what it means to live in the way of Jesus, and to be aware of how children make moral meaning. Given the right environment, according to Kohlberg, a child at a particular developmental phase can reason that there may be nothing wrong with a heinous act if it is has no negative consequences or if it's condoned by an authority figure. This is where spiritual formation meets moral development in our hand analogy, where modeling and consistency are so important for helping children to learn what is right or wrong according to God's story as lived out in particular contexts. Children need to see right action lived out in front of them, and they need to see it lived out consistently. But living morally is complicated because everywhere we turn there are moral ambiguities, issues for which God's story doesn't seem to give clear answers. As children grow morally, we can begin helping them learn how to reason ethically and theologically about these types of questions and issues.

Kohlberg argued that people could get stuck in an early stage of moral development and never proceed further than that place in terms of reasoning about right and wrong. He actually believed that many Christians get stuck along the way. In his understanding, several Christians never move beyond seeing an authority figure as the determinant for right or wrong, and they can't move on to making ethical decisions for themselves. Again, this is a place where the finger of moral development connects to the palm of spiritual formation in our hand illustration.

As we've alluded in previous chapters, our desire is for disciples of Jesus old and young to learn how to think for themselves and how to own their Christian faith. Our hope is that through family and through relationships in the community of faith, a good ethical foundation can be laid and children can learn how to make good decisions about right and wrong instead of simply following someone else's direction. When crisis hits and a person or group in authority is found to have done something wrong or inconsistent (whether a well-known scandal like Ted Haggard or Jim and Tammy Faye Bakker emerges or a local church that says they value creation care uses polystyrene plates and plastic cutlery for church picnics), those who trusted in them for the content of their own morality are thrown into disequilibrium and their trust in the person, group and even God can be damaged and broken. Children's ministry can help children move beyond believing that something is right or wrong because a human authority figure tells them so. It can guide them in learning how to make ethical decisions for themselves.

Spiritual formation. Jesus knew that spiritual formation isn't something that's separate from all other areas of human life. He ministered to the whole of persons—healing their bodies, renewing their minds, guiding their moral lives, reconciling their relationships, invigorating their souls. Human beings are whole; each aspect of our humanity affects the others. When we are caring for children in congregations or in our families, we can start seeing them as whole persons and not just disembodied souls who need to know about Jesus. We can expand our care for them and help ensure that all aspects of their being are as healthy as can be. When we seek to nurture the whole of children, we nurture them in the way God created them to be nurtured.

HOLISTIC HUMAN *BEINGS*

There's another way of thinking about holistic children's ministry. It involves helping children to follow Jesus in every area of their lives.

We've both been involved in churches, theological schools and Christian organizations where we've met folks who are incredibly involved in the life of the congregation but don't seem to act like a Christian, like a follower of Jesus, in the other areas of their lives. In fact, the phenomenon of the "Sunday Christian" is so prevalent that there's even a short Wikipedia entry about it: "A Sunday Christian or Sunday morning Christian (also Once-a-weeker) is a derisive term used to refer to someone who typically attends Christian church services on Sundays while not strictly adhering to the doctrines or rules of the religion."[5]

"Sunday Christians" are people who compartmentalize their faith so that they only seem to try to live into the way of Jesus when they're with other Christians. Christianity becomes more like an exclusive, secret club where rituals, beliefs and practices are only lived out when there aren't any outsiders around. And while it may be easy to judge Sunday Christians, we sympathize with them. In a world that can seem inhospitable and even downright hostile to Christianity, it's easy to check all markers of Christianity when we leave church. Now, we don't want to encourage a martyr complex. But David Kinnaman's research shows that even though many of us are trying to demonstrate a loving, caring, hospitable, peaceful and just Christianity, many people don't look very favorably on Christianity.[6] So we can understand why some folks want to avoid coming out of the Christian closet.

But what some people forget is that naming oneself as a Christian and living as a disciple of Jesus are completely different things. Jesus doesn't call us to put a fish on our bumpers, to use the Shepherd's Guide instead of the phone book and to sport all sorts of merchandise with misinterpreted Bible verses used in "inspirational" ways. Jesus doesn't call us to be a Christian. He calls us to *be* Christian in the earliest sense of the word, to follow him like "little Christs." He doesn't say "Come, call yourself a Christian." He says "Come, follow me" (Mt 4:19).

Holistic children's ministry, then, considers the way children live out their faith in the whole of their lives. This is why a growing number of churches are self-identifying as holistic *and* missional. To be holistic means to live in the way of Jesus, to work for justice and peace, to be the hands and feet of Jesus in every area of their lives. Being a missional Christian—in the broad sense of the word—means being holistic. Many faith communities who are living into new forms of Christian faith hold to a holistic view of the gospel, one that addresses the needs of the world, that is engaged in the wider community and seeks to join God in healing our broken world.[7]

Holistic Christianity means following Jesus in all areas of life. It means living as a disciple beyond the walls of our local churches. It means connecting our faith with our everyday lives. It means joining God in seeking first the kingdom wherever we find ourselves.

We argued earlier that a schooling-instructional model isn't fit for the tasks of children's ministry and spiritual formation as we see them. It doesn't seem to us to be a very helpful approach for nurturing children to live in the way of Jesus in every aspect of their life. When children are set apart from worship services, when they're taught to learn answers instead of ask questions, when they don't have relationships across generations and when they learn *about* God's story without learning to live this story, a ecclesial culture is created that nurtures Sunday Christians. When children's ministry isn't connected to the rest of the congregation, when what children learn isn't connected to their lives and when Bible stories aren't set within God's grand narrative of justice, peace and hope, it's easy for children to see Christianity as something that's not connected to the rest of their lives.

So how do we help children embrace a holistic Christianity? How can we move from forming children into Sunday Christians to cultivating a generation of disciples who follow Jesus with the whole of their being? The answers to these questions are as diverse and numerous as the contexts we minister in. But we'll offer three ideas that we believe to be particularly helpful.

Connect. We're sure that we've all been there. We've all been at that church listening to a sermon or at that Christian education class hearing someone teach about the Bible. And at the end of the message or lesson, we walk away wondering how what we heard mattered to the rest of our lives.

Children's ministry can easily become like this. We might teach children about a particular Bible story and we might have fun games with theological messages during vacation Bible school. But too often what churches teach children fails to connect with the realities of their lives. They learn that David was after God's heart, that God protected Noah and his family, and that Jesus turned water into wine at what can seem like a poorly planned wedding reception. But is what we teach and do with children really connected to their lives? Sadly, the answer is often no.

When we seek to help children live a holistic Christianity, what we do with them in our congregations and our ministries connects to what they're doing in the rest of their lives. This doesn't mean that we pass out WWJD bracelets or pencils with Bible verses on them. It means building bridges between God's story and our stories. And a great way to do this is to invite children to ask questions, which we discussed in chapter six. When children are encouraged to freely ask questions about what they're learning, seeing, doing and experiencing within our faith communities and families, they do so out of the contexts of their lives.

Instead of building factories for producing Sunday Christians, children's ministry can tear down walls that separate the child's church life and the rest of the child's life. When we begin to demolish the Christian silo, all the seeds of Christianity that were stored in it scatter, take root and grow in other areas of children's lives.

Get out. When we build connections between the what children do
at church and what they do in the rest of their lives, we let children
know that it's okay (even vital) to bring their whole selves to church.
But we can't stop at this. We who teach, lead and minister with children
can make an effort to get out of the church and be involved in other
areas of children's lives. We can go to their soccer games, dance recitals, science fairs and school band concerts. We can volunteer in
their schools and community centers. There are countless ways that we
can get involved in the lives of our young people outside the walls of
the church.

And this doesn't apply only to children's pastors and Sunday school
teachers. If children are full members of the faith community, then the
senior pastor is their pastor too. If children form mentoring relationships with adults, then these mentors are their caregivers too. Getting
involved in a child's life beyond local churches rests on more than just
the children's minister. It rests on all who act as spiritual guides to
young people.

We imagine some people might respond to this idea by saying that
their lives are so busy already that they can't imagine doing all this
for every child in their church's children's ministries. This raises an
important question. And our response would be that no one needs
do it all!

We know of one associate pastor of a mid-sized congregation with a
junior high class of about twenty kids. She makes sure that every year
she attends one extracurricular activity for each child. She goes to one
of Mohammed's baseball games, one of Tanya's piano recitals, one of
Steven's school plays. This allows her to show these tweens that, as their
pastor, she cares about the whole of their lives and not just when they
show up on Sunday mornings.

And who says it's all up to the pastor? Children's ministry fosters
participation, hospitality and relationships with all sorts of people in
faith communities. What if we encouraged mentors to really take an
interest in the whole life of their young mentee? What if mentors made
commitments to go to their mentee's graduations, concerts, soccer
games and talent shows on a regular basis? What if they covenanted to

show what it means to practice holistic Christianity by volunteering with their mentees at a homeless shelter, refugee house or other organization every week? When this happens, the daunting responsibility of getting involved in young people's lives is shared among many caring adults in a faith community.

And let's not forget about the formative power of peer relationships. Imagine what it might mean for young people if they band together to become involved in their lives together beyond the walls of the church. As they do life together, they would be encouraged by one another to walk in the way of Jesus wherever life takes them, engaging with one another and with those who are not part of the Christian faith in ways that help them to allow their ongoing quest to follow Jesus infiltrate the whole of their being.

When we have broad views of church, being a community of faith means getting out of our local churches and doing life together.

Be realistic. When we encourage young people to become people who seek to follow Jesus in every area of their lives, we need to remember that we're all only human. No matter how much time and energy we dedicate into living as holistic disciples, we're going to make mistakes. It's important that we remind young people that, as hard as they may try, they won't live perfectly in the way of Jesus. This is why many congregations include a prayer of confession as part of worship services.

But we can help children see that our mistakes are not reasons to be discouraged. On the contrary, our successes—no matter how infrequent or miniscule—are reasons to be hopeful. We can help children acknowledge mistakes while celebrating successes on the journey to walk as Jesus' disciples in the whole of their lives. Tony Campolo once admitted that "Living with this kind of hyperawareness of the world around me, and the people in that world, and the pain of other people, is exhausting. I cannot do that all the time."[8] Living in the way of Jesus is a vocation that paradoxically is a constant journey and one that cannot be accomplished all of the time. Loving our neighbors doesn't happen all of the time. But it does happen.

QUESTIONS FOR CONSIDERATION

1. In what ways does your church encourage healthy physical, intellectual, emotional, social and moral development in children?

2. What aspects of children's development (physical, social, etc.) seem to be missing in your ministry? What concrete steps can you take to include them?

3. How does your church nurture faith that goes beyond the formation of Sunday Christians?

4. How can you help children live as disciples of Jesus beyond the walls of the church?

12

The End of
Children's Ministry

It's not about what it is.
It's about what it can become.

THE ONCE-LER, *THE LORAX*

◨ ◨ ◨

WE BEGAN CHAPTER ONE WITH A STORY about Ivy leaning
on a counter as she read a pamphlet for a seminar that—to her
surprise—turned out to be about building children's ministry in ways
that attract outsiders to local churches.

A decade after Ivy was flipping through this pamphlet in the Midwest,
Dave was serving as a children's pastor at a mid-sized church in Ontario. He was hired to create programs for children in the neighborhood
for times when the kids were on holidays from school—summer day
camps, March break programs and other outreach events. Since these
programs met a need in the community, parents swarmed to sign their
kids up. In fact, the community embraced these programs faster than
the congregation did. So while children were coming out of the
woodwork, Dave couldn't recruit enough volunteers and eventually
had to cap the registration. To his surprise the senior pastor was upset
with this decision. Despite the fact that he told Dave upon his hiring
that he was there to minister to the children in the neighborhood, he

said that putting a cap on registration meant that fewer children would be able to attend and fewer neighborhood parents would show up to test the Sunday service waters.

We said in chapter one that this idea of doing children's ministry to recruit their parents doesn't sit well with us. There's something inherently wrong with using ministry with children to attain a primary goal other than the spiritual formation of children, of helping children live as disciples of Jesus. But in our imperfect world and our imperfect churches, our own agendas can co-opt children's spiritual formation. Over the years we've seen all sorts of ways that leaders, churches and parents use children's ministry initiatives to meet their own needs and, in so doing, turn it into something less than we believe it should be. And we admit that over the years we've sometimes made children's ministry more about us and our needs than about nurturing children. The following are just a few scenarios of how this can play out.

- The pastor who wants her church to have fun and entertaining children's ministry programs so it can act as a gateway into the church for the people who really matter—their parents.

- The parent who needs child care or a respite from the struggles of raising children and sees church-based programs as ways to get a break from his kids.

- The Sunday school teacher who wants to feel like he's making a difference in someone's life by passing on his faith to the younger generation.

- The senior who wants children to be involved in church so she knows that her beloved graying parish of which she's been a part for the past eighty years isn't doomed to close its doors forever.

- The high school student who volunteers in children's ministry initiatives in order to beef up his resume and college applications.

We don't want to imply that these intentions are bad, that these reasons for being involved in ministry with children in whatever shape and scope are utterly problematic. Remember the family we introduced in chapter eleven? They began a journey of ongoing discipleship because the boys loved coming to the summer day camps that Dave ran. What began as a sort of child care for this family became an ongoing process of Christian formation in a local faith community. We can tell all sorts of stories of how struggling families received much-needed respite when their children went to church events with the neighbors, how retired teachers continued to find joy in exercising their gifts by teaching Sunday school, how knowing that younger generations were being involved in the life of the church gave seniors a sense of peace that their embers of their church would continue to glow—and maybe even reignite.

We're not against any of these outcomes. We want to see families make commitments to journey together in the way of Jesus. We want the seniors in our congregations to bless young generations, to pass the baton of faith, and to rest assured that their faith communities will continue to thrive after their time. We want churches to help parents who, due to financial poverty or what Pamela Couture calls "the poverty of tenuous connections," need some form of child care in order to have even a few moments to themselves.[1] We want to help teens and young adults learn what it means to give back to their communities. And we want those who make commitments to help form young people in faith to know that what they do matters, that their efforts make a difference in the lives of children.

But if these goals move to the foreground, it's problematic. When they eclipse the ultimate purposes of ministry with children, when the spiritual formation of young people takes a back seat to other goals and purposes, children's ministry becomes a means to another end. When, for whatever reason, we hijack and co-opt children's ministry so that it meets our needs rather than nurturing the spiritual capacities of children, we lose sight of the task of children's ministry we outlined in chapter one (and elaborated on throughout this book)—to serve children, to minister with children.

Ministry with children is an end in and of itself. The reason we seek to nurture children's spiritual formation ought to be first and foremost about helping young people become committed followers of Jesus. There's certainly room for other goals, purposes and needs, like wanting to feel like we're making a difference and helping to ensure that our faith communities live longer than we do. But when these needs move from the sidelines to center field, when they become primary instead of secondary purposes, then the actual needs and lives of the children with whom we minister are pushed aside and replaced by our own agendas.

Jesus took children from the sidelines and placed them on his lap. He made them the center of his attention when they were with him.

But even the passages that show that Jesus saw children as ends to themselves can easily be co-opted for our adult-centric purposes. Almost every time we've heard a sermon about Jesus blessing the children (Mt 19:13-15; Mk 10:13-16; Lk 18:15-17), we've witnessed pastors and priests fail to follow Jesus' lead in calling children to the center of our attention. Instead, the needs of adults remain in center stage and the unnamed children in this passage are used as means for learning about the spiritual lives of adults. We exegete, deconstruct and ruminate on Jesus' words—"Whoever doesn't welcome God's kingdom like a child will never enter it" (Mk 10:15)—so that we adults can know what this passage means for us, what it means about faith in general (read, adult faith). If the faith of children is open, unassuming and meek, then we should try to have such faith. But when we view this story in this sort of way, we miss the face value of Jesus' words and actions. It's easy to assume that Jesus was using these children as an object lesson for the benefit of his (adult) disciples. But maybe he was just giving them the love, attention and blessing that they deserved simply because they were children, because they too were disciples in training. When we try to make this passage more than it is, when we try to see how Jesus' ministry with children can serve our lives, we can lose sight of that truth that's staring us right in the face.

A New Kind of Ecclesial Culture

Throughout this book we've proposed ways of doing ministry with children that keep spiritual formation at the center of our vision. And we've covered much ground. While we don't consider this book to be a fully comprehensive guide for children's spiritual formation (since there's always more to say), we believe that we've spun a web of ideas and practices that work together to create a new kind of ecclesial culture, one that engages children and all of us in being formed as disciples of Jesus within churches old and new that are committed to following Jesus in the contemporary world.

The image of a web speaks of interconnectedness, of strands and networks linked together in balanced tension. Each of the ideas we've included in this book intersects with the others in order to build a solid foundation for children's spiritual formation. When one strand is broken, the strength of the web is compromised. The web might still do its job, but it does so in less-than-ideal ways. But when all strands are strong, when they all intersect and connect with each other, they create an incredibly strong structure.

Let's focus on the topic of forming children into justice seekers (chap. 10) for a moment. When we see the ideas and practices we've addressed as a web, then the notion of cultivating a spirit of justice seeking in young people intersects with ideas in other chapters. One way to help children develop an unquenchable thirst for justice, peace and reconciliation is to teach them God's story (chap. 5), a story oriented toward justice, peace and compassion.[2] God's story is bent toward hope and restoration. It is a narrative in which God shows mercy and compassion, and Jesus proclaims justice to all people. And when young people realize that the story isn't over and that they're protagonists in this epic narrative of shalom, they can take up God's challenge to act justly, love mercy and walk humbly.

But in several episodes of God's story, justice doesn't seem to be the order of the day. God's story may be oriented toward peace and justice, but it's a tale riddled with violence. God may have told Israel that they should not kill, but in other parts of the Bible God seems to condone (and even encourage) violence. What are we to make of the fact that the Old Testament portrays a God who instructs Israel to kill, colonize and plunder? As we seek to help children develop a thirst for justice by learning God's story, we may encounter their questions about the violence in the Bible. So it's important to allow space for children to share their questions and their doubts (chap. 6), not only about God's story but also about how we can work for justice in the world. Joy Carroll Wallis and Jim Wallis once told of how their son, Luke, wrestled with complexities and doubts surrounding justice in a prayer one night: "Lord I pray for the 30,000 children who will die tomorrow. . . . Please don't let them die. . . . Well, I know that's not possible, so please let them have their best day ever. . . . But of course it won't be their best day ever. . . . so . . . Lord, please help us to stop this from happening."[3]

The task of nurturing a spirit of justice seeking in children intersects with other ideas as well. When children are able to participate in the practices of a faith community (chap. 7), when they help collect the weekly offering, when they sing hymns of peace and justice, when they serve alongside adults at soup kitchens, when they go door-to-door collecting canned food with their faith community, they are learning what it means to act justly in their corners of the globe.

We said in chapter ten that nurturing a desire for justice in children can involve providing opportunities for them to get to know all sorts of different people. So when ministry with children (and faith communities in general) practice radical hospitality (chap. 8), they can become places where children rub shoulders with people who are different than they are—who practice a different faith tradition, who come from different countries, who speak different languages, who have families that don't look like their own and so on. We can both attest to the power of personal relationships with those struggling against oppression, prejudice and poverty to bend our hearts toward justice.

In chapter nine we addressed the immense value of intergenerational relationships as a formative influence on children's lives (and adults' lives too!). When children get to know adult Christians who have more experience in working for justice in the world, they can learn much about what it means to seek peace and pursue justice. Imagine the formative power of an adult mentor who gradually guides a child or teenager in the quest to repair the world. Perhaps it begins as the mentor tells the young person about her volunteer work with Habitat for Humanity. Over time she can share about the problem of homelessness, teaching her mentee that it's a much more complex issue than people often believe. Later, as they are on their way to pick up some ice cream cones at a downtown shop, this mentor can model what it means to treat the homeless people they encounter with humanity, dignity and respect. And maybe the time will even come when the mentor invites the young person (with permission of a parent or guardian) to join her in helping to build a house on a particular Saturday morning. This intergenerational relationship would help the young person gradually and appropriately learn about and experience justice seeking in her own community.

These are just a few examples of how the ideas and practices we laid down in this book intersect with each other. There nodes of connection are many. But when we see all that we do to nurture children on their walk to follow in the way of Jesus as intertwined, we begin building a new kind of ecclesial culture, one that honors and blesses the children in our midst as Jesus did many centuries ago.

A Not-So-Popular Culture

But this new kind of ecclesial culture isn't always welcome in faith communities.

Not too long ago Dave was speaking to a group of young adults who were training to serve as camp counselors for the summer. He saw an opportunity to scratch two items off his to-do list at once and decided to run some of the ideas from this book by them and get some feedback. As he sat on the porch with these thirty young people, he shared about the importance of seeing children as spiritual (chap. 2) and of helping them be formed as disciples (chap. 3). He mentioned some practices for embracing questions and diving into doubt (chap. 6), creating spaces of radical hospitality (chap. 8) and building friendships across generations (chap. 9).

After his presentation, Dave asked the young adults if they had any questions or comments they'd like to share. One of the first hands raised belonged to a young man at the back of the group who appeared to be a veteran counselor. He thanked Dave for sharing his ideas and said that they resonated with him and his experiences as a counselor in past summers. But then he said something that Dave didn't anticipate: "Many of the parents of the campers are sending them to camp because we're a Christian camp and they want their kids to learn things about God while they're here. So if we spend the summer getting kids to ask good questions and sharing doubts with each other, their parents are going to be upset with us. How do we talk to kids about doubt and uncertainty when their parents may want us to teach them what they believe Christianity says to be definitely true?"

This question hits home to both of us. We've been there, trying to balance the expectations of other individuals—parents, families, pastors, board members, teachers and children—with our own beliefs, values and visions for spiritual formation. And we've experienced times when the powers that be have run up against our agendas for children's spiritual formation.

Of the many different demographic groups represented in typical congregations, children are one of the groups with the least power. They aren't usually members, so they don't have a vote (and a voice) in the shape of the community. They don't typically sit on boards, councils or committees, so their ideas remain marginal to the leadership of the church. They don't make large financial contributions (although we're sure many of them would consider giving their $5 weekly allowance to be a large contribution), so they aren't seen to add any financial value to the congregation.

And since children themselves don't tend to have power in the church, children's ministry can easily become more about appeasing the agendas of those with power (pastors, parents, volunteer teachers, ministry leaders, denominational leaders, parish council members) than about nurturing the spiritual lives of children in appropriate and authentic ways. As much as we may try to resist caving in to the sometimes problematic views of powerbrokers, well-intentioned as they may be, sometimes we may face the choice of shaping up or shipping out.

When we turn our focus to children and do what we believe is best for their spiritual formation, it's quite possible that we may upset the status quo in the process. When we begin to ask difficult yet important questions about how we as a community ought to shape children in the way of Jesus, we can upset the often delicate ecclesial environment that powerbrokers and other adults hold dear. When we begin to explore how to include children in worship, some adults may complain that their presence is getting in the way of the only time they get each week for quiet reflection. When we encourage children to ask questions, and when we take the questions they ask seriously, pastors and teachers may become concerned that children aren't learning biblical truths that they know so well. When we teach children about justice and injustice in our world, parents can get upset with us for teaching them about unpleasant things that "children shouldn't have to know about," forgetting that millions of children lack the luxury of not knowing about injustice.

The ecclesial culture that we imagine in this book isn't always popular. Although we believe it honors children's spiritual lives and their ability to think theologically, other people may not find it helpful. Although we believe the practices we've shared help create a rich environment for forming children into disciples of Jesus, we've run across more than a few people who think we've gone astray from how to teach children about what really matters. And even though many times we've found much support as we sought to put feet on these ideas over the years, at other times we've had to struggle and push to put our vision for children's ministry into practice.

We don't tell all of this to invoke fear or discouragement. We simply want to soberly share the reality that children's ministry in the way of Jesus—at least as we have imagined it in this book—can be difficult for some people to accept. We've learned through trial and error that, as much as we've spoken about the education of children, adults in congregations often need to be educated as well. We need to honestly share with them about how we seek to form young disciples in our churches. When we do this, we can create spaces for thinking *with* one another about what really matters to our children's spiritual formation and how we can empower them to be authentic, radical and loving followers of Jesus who seek first God's kingdom.

This may not be an easy task. Often it involves a re-education that seeks to dislodge problematic assumptions about children, faith and church that are common in the society we live in and the churches where we worship. While our hope is that some adults will quickly become our allies, it may take some time for others to come on board. Remember that even Jesus wasn't able to get his disciples to understand the importance of children the first time. All three Synoptic Gospels show that not long after Jesus took a child in his arms and said that "Whoever welcomes one such child in my name welcomes me" (Mt 18:2-5; Mk 9:36-37; Lk 9:47-48), the disciples rebuked people for bringing little children to Jesus (Mt 19:13-15; Mk 10:13-16; Lk 18:15-17). We can almost see Jesus smacking his head in disbelief, wondering if his disciples were even listening to him.

A couple of months ago Ivy was at a conference and found herself late one evening sitting with a group of people discussing church and children's ministry. Two of the women she was sitting with had read her books and asked, "So what does children's ministry look like at Ivy Beckwith's church?" Ivy panicked as she quickly thought about how to answer that question. The truth is that Ivy's children's ministry is not a perfect picture of the things she writes about. She decided to tell the women the truth, which is what she did.

As much as Ivy would like to provide a perfect model of her ideas in her everyday ministry, she still runs up against the concerns that we outline in this chapter. But what is important is that she is not satisfied with this, and that the issues we address in this book are always forefront in her mind as she plans activities and events or simply talks with children and parents. She is fortunate to be in a place that allows her to experiment and continue to work out and play with the ideas posited in these pages. And she continues to hope that she is laying a foundation for new kinds of children's ministry.

Within the new kind of ecclesial culture we imagine in this book, children can be in the way. One the one hand, they can grow up living "in the way of Jesus." But on the other hand, they can get in the way of the assumptions and expectations of adults—pastors, parents, congregants, board members and others. And when children get in the way of others, rather than growing through encounters with difference, some people can respond with hostility. It's important for those of us who imagine new ways of ministering with children to be prepared to run up against folks who react negatively to changes that we try to implement. When we're prepared for pushback, we can be better poised to engage criticisms, using some of them to improve our ministry with children and allowing other, less-helpful criticisms to slide off our backs.

HOPE-FILLED CHILDREN'S MINISTRY

As much as we've faced our share of challenges on this journey of helping children walk in the way of Jesus, we've found good friends, allies and coconspirators who encourage us and advocate for us and the children we seek to nurture. As much as we've had cause to grieve defeat, we've had even more cause to celebrate successes. We've learned the importance of finding colleagues, supporters, mentors and allies who can offer encouragement and support—as well as constructive criticism—when needed.

We have been dealing with these challenges of implementing new kinds of children's ministry for a while now. While we have met with opposition to our ideas in some churches, we've continued to receive great support for our ideas from children's pastors and others in the trenches. We hear from people who resonate with what we have to say, people who say they've been thinking the same things for a while. This gives us hope because we believe that sooner or later these new ideas will break through and stories about the kind of children's ministry we imagine will no longer be seen as exceptional, but will be commonplace.

Advocates who support us and moments of celebration give us cause to hope. They ignite our passion and spur us on to take up the challenge of walking with young disciples on the spiritual journey. The kind of children's ministry we have envisioned in this book is like the rocky coast of Newfoundland—incredibly beautiful and incredibly treacherous at one and the same time.

But when we remember that God is already at work in the lives of the children in our midst, we can walk with children singing songs of hope. When we recall the promise that there's a new world coming and that it's already here, we can take up the challenges before us knowing that God is doing a new thing.

As we've walked the spiritual journey with children, as we've formed them as they've formed us, young people have given us much cause to hope. When they literally stop to smell the flowers, when they marvel at quiet beauty that we've been taught to ignore, and when they cry out for those who are suffering, we are overwhelmed with hope for the church—and for the world.

> Look! I'm doing a new thing;
>> now it sprouts up; don't you recognize it? (Is 43:19)

Notes

Introduction: Doing Children's Ministry Differently

[1]We're certainly not the only ones who have noticed this. A few years ago Scottie May, Beth Posterski, Catherine Stonehouse and Linda Cannell picked up on this trend as well: "Since [the missional or emerging church] movement is led by a younger generation, if the leaders have children, they are still quite young. The leaders of this movement must thoroughly consider the role their children will play in the worship experiences of their faith communities" (Scottie May, Beth Posterski, Catherine Stonehouse and Linda Cannell, *Children Matter: Celebrating Their Place in the Church, Family, and Community* [Grand Rapids: Eerdmans, 2005], p. 242).

[2]Melvin Bray shared this in an interview at the "Children, Youth, and a New Kind of Christianity" conference, Washington, DC, May 7-10, 2012.

[3]Donald Stuss, "For Better Cures, Let's Do Science Differently," *Globe and Mail*, August 6, 2012, p. A9.

Chapter 1: The Task of Children's Ministry

[1]Rolf A. Jacobsen, ed., *Crazy Talk: A Not-So-Stuffy Dictionary of Theological Terms* (Minneapolis: Augsburg, 2008), p. 116.

[2]Paulo Freire, *Pedagogy of the Oppressed*, trans. Myra Bergman Ramos, 30th anniversary ed. (New York: Continuum, 2007).

[3]John H. Westerhoff III, *Will Our Children Have Faith?* 3rd ed. (Harrisburg, PA: Morehouse, 2012).

[4]Ibid., p. 18.

[5]Ibid., p. 20.

Chapter 2: Authentic Spirituality

[1]Dave originally wrote about this in *Children's Ministry That Fits: Beyond One-Size-Fits-All Approaches to Nurturing Children's Spirituality* (Eugene, OR: Wipf & Stock, 2011).

[2]Reginald W. Bibby, with Sarah Russell and Ron Rolheiser, *The Emerging Millennials: How Canada's Newest Generation Is Responding to Change & Choice* (Lethbridge, AB: Project Canada, 2009); Christian Smith, with Patricia Snell, *Souls in Transition: The Religious and Spiritual Lives of Emerging Adults* (Oxford: Oxford

University Press, 2009); Robert Wuthnow, *After the Baby Boomers: How Twenty- and Thirty-Somethings Are Shaping the Future of American Religion* (Princeton, NJ: Princeton University Press, 2005); and Diana Butler Bass, *Christianity After Religion: The End of Church and the Birth of a New Spiritual Awakening* (New York: Harper-Collins, 2012).

[3]Bass, *Christianity After Religion*, pp. 92-93; Wuthnow, *After the Baby Boomers*, p. 134.

[4]Wuthnow, *After the Baby Boomers*, p. 131.

[5]Rebecca Nye, "Relational Consciousness and the Spiritual Lives of Children: Convergence with Children's Theory of Mind," in *Psychological Studies of Children's Spiritual and Religious Development*, ed. K. Helmut Reich et al. (Lengerich, Germany: Pabst, 1999), p. 58.

[6]Jean Vanier, "The Fragility of L'Arche and the Friendship of God," in *Living Gently in a Violent World* (Downers Grove, IL: InterVarsity Press, 2008), pp. 22-23.

[7]Karl Rahner, "Ideas for a Theology of Childhood," in *Theological Investigations* (New York: Herder & Herder, 1971), 8:48.

[8]Jean-Pierre de Caussade, *The Sacrament of the Present Moment*, trans. Kitty Muggeridge (New York: HarperOne, 1981).

[9]Joyce E. Bellous, *Educating Faith: An Approach to Christian Formation* (Toronto: Clements, 2006), p. 20.

[10]David Hay with Rebecca Nye, *The Spirit of the Child*, rev. ed. (London: Jessica Kingsley, 2006), p. 110.

[11]Ibid., pp. 94-95.

[12]Barbara Kimes Myers, *Young Children and Spirituality* (New York: Routledge, 1997), p. 11.

[13]Ibid., p. 12.

[14]Pew Forum on Religion and Public Life, "Religion Among the Millennials," February 17, 2010, www.pewforum.org/Age/Religion-Among-the-Millennials.aspx. David Kinnaman and Gabe Lyons, *unChristian: What a New Generation Really Thinks About Christianity . . . and Why It Matters* (Grand Rapids: Baker, 2007).

[15]Hay with Nye, *Spirit of the Child*, p. 9.

[16]Ibid., p. 33.

[17]David Hay, *Something There: The Biology of the Human Spirit* (Philadelphia: Templeton Foundation, 2007), p. 131.

[18]This is not to say, of course, that children can't experience God simply by learning about God. But the widespread focus on helping children gain propositional knowledge tends to assume that relationships with God are bound up with learning about God.

[19]John H. Westerhoff III, "The Church's Contemporary Challenge: Assisting Adults to Mature Spiritually *with* Their Children" (presentation at the Children's Spirituality Conference: Christian Perspectives, River Forest, Illinois, June 2006).

[20]Rob Bell, *Velvet Elvis: Repainting the Christian Faith* (Grand Rapids: Zondervan, 2005), p. 32.

[21]Christian Smith's research found that American teenagers typically lack adequate

language for talking about religion, faith and spirituality. Christian Smith, with Melinda Lundquist Denton, *Soul Searching: The Religious and Spiritual Lives of American Teenagers* (Oxford: Oxford University Press, 2005), pp. 131-33, 267-68.

Chapter 3: Formational Discipleship

[1]Gretchen Wolff Pritchard, *Offering the Gospel to Children* (Cambridge, MA: Cowley, 1992), pp. 140-41.

[2]John Wall, *Ethics in Light of Childhood* (Washington, DC: Georgetown University Press, 2010), p. 19.

[3]Ibid., p. 29.

[4]David E. Fitch, *The Great Giveaway: Reclaiming the Mission of the Church from Big Business, Parachurch Organizations, Psychotherapy, Consumer Capitalism, and Other Modern Maladies* (Grand Rapids: Baker, 2005), p. 186.

[5]Ellen Charry, "Countering a Malforming Culture: Christian Theological Formation of Adolescents in North America," in *Nurturing Child and Adolescent Spirituality: Perspectives from the World's Religious Traditions*, ed. Karen Marie Yust et al. (Lanham, MD: Rowman & Littlefield, 2006), p. 438.

[6]Joyce Ann Mercer, *Welcoming Children: A Practical Theology of Childhood* (St. Louis: Chalice, 2005), p. 173.

[7]Ibid., p. 176.

[8]Ivy has wrestled with this along her journey of discipleship. For a time she went through a hardcore stage of calling herself a "follower of Jesus" rather than identifying as a Christian. But now she prefers to identify as "Christian" (adjective/adverb) rather than "a Christian" (noun).

[9]John H. Westerhoff III, *Will Our Children Have Faith?* 3rd ed. (Harrisburg, PA: Morehouse, 2012), p. 141.

[10]John H. Westerhoff III, "The Church's Contemporary Challenge: Assisting Adults to Mature Spiritually *with* Their Children," in *Nurturing Children's Spirituality: Christian Perspectives and Best Practices*, ed. Holly Catterton Allen (Eugene, OR: Cascade, 2008), p. 359.

[11]Pamela Couture offers a succinct definition of a disciple: "one who learns the way of life that Jesus taught" (Pamela Couture, *Child Poverty: Love, Justice, and Social Responsibility* [St. Louis: Chalice, 2007], p. 162). She reminds us that Jesus' discipleship was (and still is) countercultural, and she notes that after being apprenticed into Jesus' way of life, Jesus' first disciples began to apprentice others.

[12]Eddie Gibbs and Ryan K. Bolger, *Emerging Churches: Creating Christian Community in Postmodern Cultures* (Grand Rapids: Baker Academic, 2005), p. 90.

[13]To learn about how Jesus apprenticed his disciples into his way of life, see David M. Csinos, "'Come, Follow Me': Apprenticeship in Jesus' Approach to Education," *Religious Education* 105, no. 1 (2010): 45-62.

[14]Rob Bell, *Velvet Elvis: Repainting the Christian Faith* (Grand Rapids: Zondervan, 2005), p. 134.

[15]Mary Elizabeth Moore, *Teaching as a Sacramental Act* (Cleveland: Pilgrim, 2004), p. 12.

[16]Mike King, *Presence-Centered Youth Ministry: Guiding Students into Spiritual Formation* (Downers Grove, IL: InterVarsity Press, 2006), p. 68.

[17]Westerhoff, "The Church's Contemporary Challenge," p. 365.

Chapter 4: Vibrant Theologies

[1]David E. Fitch, *The Great Giveaway: Reclaiming the Mission of the Church from Big Business, Parachurch Organizations, Psychotherapy, Consumer Capitalism, and Other Modern Maladies* (Grand Rapids: Baker, 2005).

[2]Ibid., p. 187.

[3]John H. Westerhoff III, "A Catechetical Way of Doing Theology," in *Theology and Religious Education*, ed. N. H. Thompson (Birmingham: Religious Education Press, 1982), p. 218.

[4]These perspectives can be found in Marcia J. Bunge, "The Child, Religion, and the Academy: Developing Robust Theological and Religious Understandings of Children and Childhood," *Journal of Religion* 86, no. 4 (2006): 549-79.

[5]Ibid., p. 563.

[6]Bonnie J. Miller-McLemore, *Let the Children Come: Reimagining Childhood from a Christian Perspective* (San Francisco: Jossey-Bass, 2003), pp. 74-75.

[7]Vigen Guroian, "The Ecclesial Family: John Chrysostom on Parenthood and Children," in *The Child in Christian Thought*, ed. Marcia J. Bunge (Grand Rapids: Eerdmans, 2001), p. 62.

[8]Karl Rahner, "Ideas for a Theology of Childhood," in *Theological Investigations*, vol. 8 (New York: Herder & Herder, 1971).

[9]Judith M. Gundry-Volf, "The Least and the Greatest: Children in the New Testament," in Bunge, *Child in Christian Thought*, p. 29.

[10]Bunge, "Child, Religion, and the Academy," p. 567.

[11]Pamela Couture, *Child Poverty: Love, Justice, and Social Responsibility* (St. Louis: Chalice, 2007).

[12]John H. Westerhoff III, "Changing Times, Changing Responses" (presentation at the "Children, Youth, and a New Kind of Christianity" conference, Washington, DC, May 8, 2012). This is a view of heresy that he offered in an introduction to the revised edition of *Will Our Children Have Faith?* (John H. Westerhoff III, *Will Our Children Have Faith?* 3rd ed. [Harrisburg, PA: Morehouse, 2012], pp. xi, 46).

[13]Bunge, "Child, Religion, and the Academy," p. 568.

[14]Miller-McLemore, *Let the Children Come*, p. 22.

[15]Keith Graber Miller, "Complex Innocence, Obligatory Nurturance, and Parental Vigilance: 'The Child' in the Work of Menno Simons," in Bunge, *Child in Christian Thought*.

[16]Karen Ward, "The Emerging Church and Communal Theology," in *Listening to the Beliefs of Emerging Churches: Five Perspectives*, ed. Robert Webber (Grand Rapids: Zondervan, 2007).

[17]Bonnie J. Miller-McLemore, *In the Midst of Chaos: Caring for Children as Spiritual Practice* (San Francisco: Jossey-Bass, 2007), p. 18.

[18]Quoted from an email to the editor, in response to David M. Csinos, "Children in the Church: How Do We Welcome Them?" *Faith Today*, Jan-Feb 2011, pp. 18-22.

[19]Scottie May, Katie Stemp and Grant Burns, "Children's Place in the New Forms of Church: An Exploratory Survey of These Forms' Ministry with Children and Families," in *Understanding Children's Spirituality: Theology, Research, and Practice*, ed. Kevin E. Lawson (Eugene, OR: Cascade, 2012), p. 252.

[20]Scottie May et al., *Children Matter: Celebrating Their Place in the Church, Family, and Community* (Grand Rapids: Eerdmans, 2005), p. 52.

[21]Joyce Ann Mercer, *Welcoming Children: A Practical Theology of Childhood* (St. Louis: Chalice, 2005), p. 142.

Chapter 5: Living Stories

[1]Thomas King, *The Truth About Stories: A Native Narrative* (Toronto: Anansi, 2003), p. 2.

[2]Phyllis Tickle, *The Great Emergence: How Christianity Is Changing and Why* (Grand Rapids: Baker, 2008), p. 34.

[3]King, *Truth About Stories*, pp. 9-10.

[4]Brian McLaren, *A New Kind of Christianity: Ten Questions That Are Transforming the Faith* (New York: HarperOne, 2010).

[5]Peter Enns, *Telling God's Story: Instructor Text and Teaching Guide* (Charles City, VA: Olive Branch, 2010), p. 7.

[6]See Vigen Guroian, "The Ecclesial Family: John Chrysostom on Parenthood and Family," in *The Child in Christian Thought*, ed. Marcia J. Bunge (Grand Rapids: Zondervan, 2001), p. 75; and Mary Ann Hinsdale, "'Infinite Openness to the Infinite': Karl Rahner's Contribution to Modern Catholic Thought on the Child," in Bunge, *Child in Christian Thought*, p. 439.

[7]Brian D. McLaren, *Why Did Jesus, Moses, the Buddha, and Mohammed Cross the Road? Christian Identity in a Multi-Faith World* (New York: Jericho, 2012), pp. 194-95. McLaren writes about the appropriateness of picking and choosing Bible passages that advocate wholeness, reconciliation and solidarity—a tradition that has been passed down to us by Jesus and leaders of the early church. For more about this see chapter 22 in ibid.

[8]Suzanne Collins, *Mockingjay* (New York: Scholastic, 2010), p. 389.

[9]Brian McLaren, *The Story We Find Ourselves In: Further Adventures of a New Kind of Christian* (San Francisco: Jossey-Bass, 2003).

[10]Brian K. Blount, *Revelation: A Commentary* (Louisville: Westminster John Knox, 2009), p. 397.

[11]N. T. Wright, "How Can the Bible Be Authoritative?" *Vox Evangelica* 21 (1991), http://ntwrightpage.com/Wright_Bible_Authoritative.htm.

[12]Ivy Beckwith, *Formational Children's Ministry: Shaping Children Using Story, Ritual, and Relationship* (Grand Rapids: Baker, 2010), p. 41.

[13]James W. Fowler, *Stages of Faith: The Psychology of Human Development and the Quest for Meaning* (San Francisco: Harper & Row, 1981), p. 149.

[14]Peter Enns, *Telling God's Story: A Parents' Guide to Teaching the Bible* (Charles City, VA: Olive Branch, 2010), pp. 12-13.

[15]*Project-Based Learning for Junior Youth* (Breslau, Ontario: Breslau Mennonite Church, n.d.).

[16]John Paul Lederach, *The Moral Imagination: The Art and Soul of Building Peace* (Oxford: Oxford University Press, 2005), p. 147.

Chapter 6: Honest Questions

[1]John H. Westerhoff III, *Will Our Children Have Faith?* 3rd ed. (Harrisburg, PA: Morehouse, 2012), p. 17.

[2]Parker J. Palmer, *The Courage to Teach: Exploring the Inner Landscape of a Teacher's Life* (San Francisco: Jossey-Bass, 1998), p. 63.

[3]Anne Lamott, *Plan B: Further Thoughts on Faith* (New York: Riverhead, 2005), pp. 256-57.

[4]Peter Rollins, "I Have Met the Stranger, and He Is Me," Peter Rollins (blog), March 27, 2012, http://peterrollins.net/?p=3611.

[5]Robert J. Keeley, *Helping Our Children Grow in Faith: How the Church Can Nurture the Spiritual Development of Kids* (Grand Rapids: Baker, 2008), p. 51.

[6]David Kinnaman, *You Lost Me: Why Young Christians Are Leaving Church . . . and Rethinking Faith* (Grand Rapids: Baker, 2011), p. 187.

[7]David Kinnaman and Gabe Lyons, *unChristian: What a New Generation Really Thinks About Christianity . . . and Why It Matters* (Grand Rapids: Baker, 2007), p. 31.

[8]For more about this, see Kinnaman, *You Lost Me.*

[9]Keeley, *Helping Our Children Grow in Faith,* p. 58.

[10]Westerhoff, *Will Our Children Have Faith?* pp. 96-98.

[11]Sandy Eisenberg Sasso, "The Spirituality of Parenting," interviewed by Krista Tippett, *On Being,* www.onbeing.org/program/spirituality-parenting/230/audio.

Chapter 7: Meaningful Participation

[1]Robert J. Keeley, "Step by Step: Faith Development and Faith Formation," in *Shaped by God: Twelve Essentials for Nurturing Faith in Children, Youth, and Adults,* ed. Robert J. Keeley (Grand Rapids: Faith Alive, 2010), p. 61.

[2]In fact, both of us have already written about children's participation in the wider congregation in our previous books. See Ivy Beckwith, *Postmodern Children's Ministry: Ministry to Children in the 21st Century* (Grand Rapids: Zondervan, 2004); Ivy Beckwith, *Formational Children's Ministry: Shaping Children Using Story, Ritual, and Relationship* (Grand Rapids: Baker, 2010); and David M. Csinos, *Children's Ministry That Fits: Beyond One-Size-Fits-All Approaches to Nurturing Children's Spirituality* (Eugene, OR: Wipf & Stock, 2011).

[3]Margaret Y. MacDonald, "A Place of Belonging: Perspectives on Children from Colossians and Ephesians," in *The Child in the Bible,* ed. Marcia J. Bunge (Grand Rapids: Eerdmans, 2008), p. 279.

[4]Patrick D. Miller, "That the Children May Know: Children in Deuteronomy," in Bunge, *Child in the Bible,* p. 51.

[5]Barbara Rogoff, *The Cultural Nature of Human Development* (Oxford: Oxford University Press, 2003), p. 11.

[6]Beckwith, *Postmodern Children's Ministry*; Beckwith, *Formational Children's Ministry*; and Csinos, *Children's Ministry That Fits*.

[7]Rogoff, *Cultural Nature of Human Development*, p. 25.

[8]Jean Lave and Etienne Wenger, *Situated Learning: Legitimate Peripheral Participation* (Cambridge: Cambridge University Press, 1991).

[9]Rogoff, *Cultural Nature of Human Development*, p. 139.

[10]Ibid., p. 285.

[11]Brian McLaren, "Christian Faith (and) the Next Generation," a presentation at the "Children, Youth, and a New Kind of Christianity" conference, Washington, DC, May 7, 2012.

[12]Joyce Ann Mercer, *Welcoming Children: A Practical Theology of Childhood* (St. Louis: Chalice, 2005), p. 2.

[13]David Ng and Virginia Thomas, *Children in the Worshiping Community* (Atlanta: John Knox, 1981), p. 16.

[14]Carla Barnhill, "The Postmodern Parent: Shifting Paradigms for the Ultimate Act of Re-Creation," in *An Emergent Manifesto of Hope*, ed. Doug Pagitt and Tony Jones (Grand Rapids: Baker, 2007), p. 56.

[15]Mercer, *Welcoming Children*, p. 235.

Chapter 8: Radical Hospitality

[1]Howard Gardner, *Frames of Mind: The Theory of Multiple Intelligences* (New York: Basic, 2011).

[2]*Big Business*, dir. Jim Abrahams, 1988.

[3]Karen B. Tye, *Basics of Christian Education* (St. Louis: Chalice, 2000), p. 71.

[4]Letty Russell, *Just Hospitality: God's Welcome in a World of Difference*, ed. J. Shannon Clarkson and Kate M. Ott (Louisville: Westminster John Knox, 2009), p. 19.

[5]Elizabeth F. Caldwell, *God's Big Table: Nurturing Children in a Diverse World* (Cleveland: Pilgrim, 2011), p. 86.

Chapter 9: Intergenerational Community

[1]"Developmental Assets," Search Institute, www.search-institute.org/developmental-assets. While we can debate the problematic forward-looking notion of developmental assets and their proclivity to ignore childhood and adolescence as valuable in and of themselves, the depth and breadth of the Search Institute's research means that their findings have significant implications.

[2]Christian Smith, with Melinda Lundquist Denton, *Soul Searching: The Religious and Spiritual Lives of American Teenagers* (Oxford: Oxford University Press, 2005), p. 226.

[3]Lev S. Vygotsky, *Mind in Society: The Development of Higher Psychological Processes* (Cambridge, MA: Harvard University Press, 1978), p. 86.

[4]Scottie May, Katie Stemp and Grant Burns, "Children's Place in the New Forms of Church: An Exploratory Survey of These Forms' Ministry with Children and Fam-

ilies," in *Understanding Children's Spirituality: Theology, Research, and Practice*, ed. Kevin E. Lawson (Eugene, OR: Cascade, 2012). Interestingly, the size of a church was strongly correlated with children's involvement with the entire faith community, with smaller churches being much more intergenerational than larger churches (ibid., p. 256).

[5]Eddie Gibbs and Ryan K. Bolger, *Emerging Churches: Creating Christian Community in Postmodern Cultures* (Grand Rapids: Baker Academic, 2005), pp. 97-98.

[6]Diana Garland has done some of the best work in family ministry. See Diana R. Garland, *Family Ministry: A Comprehensive Guide*, 2nd ed. (Downers Grove, IL: IVP Academic, 2012); Diana Garland, *Inside Out Families: Living the Faith Together* (Waco, TX: Baylor University Press, 2010); and Diana R. Garland, *Sacred Stories of Ordinary Families: Living the Faith in Daily Life* (San Francisco: Jossey-Bass, 2003).

[7]Holly Catterton Allen, "Nurturing Children's Spirituality in Intergenerational Christian Settings," in *Children's Spirituality: Christian Perspectives, Research, and Applications*, ed. Donald Ratcliff (Eugene, OR: Cascade, 2004), pp. 267-68.

[8]Joseph R. Myers, *The Search to Belong: Rethinking Intimacy, Community, and Small Groups* (Grand Rapids: Zondervan, 2003); Joseph R. Myers, *Organic Community: Creating a Place Where People Naturally Connect* (Grand Rapids: Baker, 2007).

[9]Joyce Ann Mercer, *Girltalk, Godtalk: Why Faith Matters to Teenage Girls—and Their Parents* (San Francisco: Jossey-Bass, 2008), p. 127.

[10]Bryan Moyer Suderman, homepage of SmallTall Music, www.smalltallmusic.com.

Chapter 10: Transformative Justice

[1]Brian D. McLaren, "Introduction: A Conversation About Justice," in *The Justice Project*, ed. Brian McLaren, Elisa Padilla and Ashley Bunting Seeber (Grand Rapids: Baker, 2009), p. 18.

[2]Craig Kielburget and Mark Kielburger, *Me to We: Finding Meaning in a Material World* (New York: Fireside, 2004), p. 228.

[3]Brian D. McLaren, *Why Did Jesus, Moses, the Buddha, and Mohammed Cross the Road? Christian Identity in a Multi-Faith World* (New York: Jericho, 2012), p. 223.

[4]Pamela Couture, *Child Poverty: Love, Justice, and Social Responsibility* (St. Louis: Chalice, 2007), p. 51.

[5]Shane Claiborne, "Becoming the Church We Dream Of," Princeton Theological Seminary, www.ptsem.edu/uploadedFiles/School_of_Christian_Vocation_and_Mission/Institute_for_Youth_Ministry/Princeton_Lectures/2010_Claiborne_Becoming.pdf, accessed March 25, 2013.

Chapter 11: Holistic Lives

[1]Doug Pagitt, *A Christianity Worth Believing: Hope-Filled, Open-Armed, Alive-and-Well Faith for the Left Out, Left Behind, and Let Down in Us All* (San Francisco: Jossey-Bass, 2008), p. 85.

[2]See Mario Beauregard and Denyse O'Leary, *The Spiritual Brain: A Neuroscientist's Case for the Existence of the Soul* (Toronto: HarperCollins, 2007); Rhawn Joseph, ed.,

NeuroTheology: Brain, Science, Spirituality, Religious Experience (San Jose, CA: University Press, 2003); Mark Graves, *Mind, Brain, and the Elusive Souls* (Aldershot, UK: Ashgate, 2008); and Barbara Bradley Hagerty, *Fingerprints of God: The Search for the Science of Spirituality* (New York: Riverhead, 2009).

[3]For a rudimentary, if somewhat outdated, introduction to this debate, see the ABC Nightline documentary "Spirituality and the Brain: Is God a Figment of the Imagination?" http://ffh.films.com/PreviewClip.aspx?id=4603.

[4]Scholars like Carol Gilligan would later take Kohlberg to task for making universal assumptions from research conducted only with male subjects in particular social locations (Carol Gilligan, *In a Different Voice: Psychological Theory and Women's Development* [Cambridge, MA: Harvard University Press, 1982]).

[5]"Sunday Christian," *Wikipedia*, http://en.wikipedia.org/wiki/Sunday_Christian.

[6]David Kinnaman and Gabe Lyons, *unChristian: What a New Generation Really Thinks About Christianity . . . and Why It Matters* (Grand Rapids: Baker, 2007).

[7]Eddie Gibbs and Ryan K. Bolger, *Emerging Churches: Creating Christian Community in Postmodern Cultures* (Grand Rapids: Baker Academic, 2005), pp. 149-50.

[8]Tony Campolo, "A Letter to My Granddaughter, Growing Up as a Christian," in *Children, Youth, and a New Kind of Christianity*, ed. David M. Csinos and Melvin Bray (Kelowna, BC: CopperHouse, 2013), p. 206.

Chapter 12: The End of Children's Ministry

[1]Pamela D. Couture, *Seeing Children, Seeing God: A Practical Theology of Children and Poverty* (Nashville: Abingdon, 2000).

[2]See David M. Csinos and Brian D. McLaren, "Breaking the Bubble Wrap," *Sojourners* 41, no. 7 (2012): 16-22.

[3]See Joy Carroll Wallis, "Let's Say Grace," in *Children, Youth, and a New Kind of Christianity*, ed. David M. Csinos and Melvin Bray (Kelowna, BC: CopperHouse, 2013).

PRAXIS

EQUIPPING LEADERS FOR MINISTRY

"...TO EQUIP HIS PEOPLE FOR WORKS OF SERVICE,
SO THAT THE BODY OF CHRIST MAY BE BUILT UP."

EPHESIANS 4:12

God has called us to ministry. But it's not enough to have a vision for ministry if you don't have the practical skills for it. Nor is it enough to do the work of ministry if what you do is headed in the wrong direction. We need both vision *and* expertise for effective ministry. We need *praxis*.

Praxis puts theory into practice. It brings cutting-edge ministry expertise from visionary practitioners. You'll find sound biblical and theological foundations for ministry in the real world, with concrete examples for effective action and pastoral ministry. Praxis books are more than the "how to" – they're also the "why to." And because *being* is every bit as important as *doing*, Praxis attends to the inner life of the leader as well as the outer work of ministry. Feed your soul, and feed your ministry.

If you are called to ministry, you know you can't do it on your own. Let Praxis provide the companions you need to equip God's people for life in the kingdom.

www.ivpress.com/praxis